Taste + Color

MARÍA VILLEGAS

Taste + Color

Direction and edition
BENJAMÍN VILLEGAS

Recipies, food styling and design
MARÍA VILLEGAS

Photography
CLAUDIA URIBE-TOURI

This book has been created, edited and
published in Colombia by
VILLEGAS ASOCIADOS S. A.
Avenida 82 No. 11-50, Interior 3
Bogotá D. C., Colombia.
Telephone (57-1) 616 1788
Fax (57-1) 616 0020
e-mail: informacion@VillegasEditores.com

© MARÍA VILLEGAS
© CLAUDIA URIBE-TOURI
© VILLEGAS EDITORES 2003

Art department
DAVID RENDÓN

English translation
JIMMY WEISKOPF

Proofreader
JENNIE KENT

Prop-styling
ANA MARÍA GONZÁLEZ-ROJAS

Cooking assistant
UXOA LANDABURU

Photography assistant
ALEJANDRO MONTOYA

All rights reserved.
No part of this book may be reproduced, stored
in a retrieval system or transmitted, in any form
or by any means, electronic, mechanical,
photocopying, recording or otherwise,
without the prior permission of Villegas Editores.

First edition
October, 2003

ISBN
958-8156-43-2

VillegasEditores.com

Thanks

No one writes a book on his or her own. If I had not been able to count on a team as solid as the one I had, the result would never have been the same. For that reason I wish to say, many times, thank you.
To my little princess Michelle, who, for the very fact of existing, leaves her mark on all we do and fills our lives with joy.
To Claudia Uribe, for her professionalism and priceless friendship, which has stood up to every test. To my grandmother, Inés, for her marvelous culinary heritage and for always being attentive to all of my escapades. To my mother, for always supporting me and sharing her beloved recipes. To my sister, Laura, who in the midst of her many activities always found time to keep up with my work and show her enthusiasm for it. To my brother, Camilo, for understanding my lack of time when he needed me so much. To my father, for continuing to believe in me, optimistically supporting my work and turning this book into a reality. To that whole gang of supportive friends made up of Uxoa, Alejandro, Ana María, Adriana, Diana, Rosa, Rosario and Juan David, for their drive, self-surrender, help and trust. To Jennie, for knowing how to wait. To David, for taking on the challenge of a new style of design with such enthusiasm and generosity and for making so many valuable contributions. To Stella, for always greeting me with a big smile, organizing my chaotic first drafts and being permanently alert to possible mistakes. To the editorial team at Villegas Editores, for sharing their space with me and making this book their own priority.
Finally, to all of the commercial firms which, with an admirable generosity and selflessness, lent us their most precious objects and marvelous products for the photographs in this book:

Anticuario Shanghai, Calle 79B # 7-82 Tel. 2495185; BB&B, Diag. 109 # 19-83 Tel. 6298045; Cachivaches, Cra. 9 # 69-26 Tel. 2498859; Carmiña Villegas, Diag. 109 # 17-37 Tel. 6207772; Christofle Pavillion, Av. 82 #11-78 L-7 Tel. 6221569; Deimos Arte, Cra. 12 #70-49 Tel. 2499868; Dupuis, Calle 79B # 7-97 Tel. 3459445; Eurolink, Calle 85 # 9-86 Tel. 2573676; Fontana Flores, Calle 79B # 7-55 Tel. 2355287; Inmaculada Concepción, Calle 57 # 3-05 Tel. 3106172; Koyomad S. A. Productos Cárnicos, Productos Koller y Kopoyo Carnes y Salsamentaria, Calle 122 # 30-12 Tel. 6196260; Lina Pardo y Colleen Bowler, potters. Calle 69 # 6-46 Tel. 2499824; María Teresa Hoyos, potter, Finca Hibernia, Chía, Tel. 8632529; Mónica de Rhodes–Hechizoo Telas, Calle 79B # 7-90 Tel. 6130510; Pacific Seafood, Transv. 24 # 82-47 Tel. 5333592; Savile Arte, Cra. 10 # 82-90 Tel. 6350675; Spazio, Calle 93B # 11A-84 L-102 Tel. 6355301; Superpollo Paisa, S. A., Calle 102 # 52-25 Tel. 6135912; Terra, Calle 72 # 6-30 Tel. 6069898; The Tea House, Cra. 14 # 80-73 Tel. 6163289; Wabi, Calle 81 # 8-28 Tel. 2129973.

This book

For you, Cocó, for all the love I feel towards you and for inventing that unexpected journey full of love, generosity and immeasurable surprises.

I had barely finished my book *À la Carte* when a sudden and, in the end, fortunate work commitment of my husband, Juan Pablo, propelled us, unexpectedly and without much time to assimilate the change, to the other side of the world – Japan.

Tokyo, the essence of the Orient, the very center of visual exuberance and wealth, the place where the exquisite takes shape and delicacy is a way of life. Tokyo, a universe that is so different and so distant that it makes any attempt to describe it impossible.

For me, occupied the whole time with my little daughter, Michelle, wandering around the city became an indispensable exercise of discovery. My natural curiosity expanded under the stimulus of so many novelties and my sensibility was constantly gratified by each finding.

Each corner of Tokyo turned out to be a prism. Everything was different there: the shop windows, the products, the packaging. Also, of course, the food, the tastes, the aromas, the restaurants, the tableware, the designs, the way the dishes are presented and served, and underlying it all, the delicacy, the subtlety, the suggestiveness, the mystery...

There is no doubt that I was in a privileged place, in a dream-like world for someone like myself, who immensely enjoys esthetic pleasures and aspires to create and recreate, to combine and transform flavors, tastes, aromas and fragrances.

I had to take advantage of my journey. The very special circumstances that surrounded my stay in Japan were made for it. My travels through China, the Philippines, Malaysia and Taiwan gave me a more complete vision of the food of that part of the world and what it truly means, as well as of the intricate fusion of culinary traditions that is implicit in it.

My eternal love for cook books was pleasantly rewarded during this time. The availability of the original ingredients joined with an irrepressible need to try my hand at combining them and the uncontrollable temptation to attempt an evocative mixture of all that I was learning from the diverse gastronomical cultures with which I had come into contact in the course of my professional training and working experience. Thus, this new book grew into existence: of recipes that are tried and tested.

On my return it was time to put my ideas into practice. I had to think up a book that would captivate the eye and pay tribute to good taste, as well as please the palate. There was no question that I would turn to my good friend, photographer Claudia Uribe, for her input.

Claudia and I began to analyze and work on a suitable design that would visually interpret the idea I had in mind: to establish a close link between the concepts of taste and color.

The book took shape – comprised of six different colors, each covering a wide range of recipes that are quick and simple to prepare and suitable for all tastes and occasions, formal and informal. In an effort to surprise and to break with the monotony of many cook books, I have included all kinds of useful culinary tips and a wide selection of ideas whose colors will grace both the dishes and your table.

I hope that all of this work, done with so much passion and love, will be reflected in the satisfaction of every person who reads and uses this book.

If it works out that way, Claudia and I will also be satisfied.

María Villegas

Contents

White

17

Green

49

Yellow

77

Orange

107

Red

143

Brown

173

Appendix

207

Glossary

Ingredients

217

Index of recipes

White

- Thai grapefruit and vermicelli salad, 18
- Squid rings with minted lime sauce, 21
- Lemongrass risotto, 23
- Easy bread rolls, 24
- Graibes, 28
- Savory biscuits, 28
- Alfajores, 29
- Lemon marmalade sandwich biscuits, 29
- Rice pudding, 30
- Sugared churros, 33
- Lychee Cocktail, 34
- Lebanese cream with mangosteens, 37
- Pavlova with coconut and lime, 38
- Old-fashioned pound-cake, 41

Green

- Green salad with walnuts and Brie, 50
- Fish ceviche with coconut milk, 53
- Mediterranean prawn croquettes, 54
- Fresh pasta with coriander, 57
- Boconccini coated with fines herbes, 60
- Vine leaf cous-cous rolls, 60
- Cucumber rolls with curried chicken, 61
- Plantain chips with guacamole, 61
- Green Thai fish kebabs, 62
- Red snapper with hummus, 65
- Asparagus and Camembert quiche, 66
- Broccoli and Béarnaise flan, 69

Yellow

- Ilo-Ilo clams, 78
- Hindustan-style chicken, 81
- Carrot and blue cheese soup, 82
- French onion soup, 85
- Fonduta in farm bread, 86
- Grated potato cakes, 90
- Creole potatoes, 90
- Potato balls, 91
- Golden brown potato slices, 91
- Cheese muffins, 93
- Bananas with coconut and spearmint, 95
- Passion fruit and white chocolate pie, 96
- Golden crêpes, 99

Orange

- Salmon and nori spring rolls, 108
- Shrimps with chili and orange, 111
- Pasta, pumpkin and Gorgonzola, 112
- Sweet-sour chicken with cashews, 115
- Tomato soup with herb wontons, 116
- Twice-baked potatoes with salmon, 118
- Prawn and crayfish bisque, 121
- Shrimp tempura with herbes butter, 122
- Spicy apricot Basmati, 124
- Tangerine mimosa, 128
- Tea with Amaretto and apricot, 128
- Goldenberry chiller, 129
- White peach Sangría, 129
- Apricot chutney, 131
- Carrot halvahs, 132
- Orange blossom crème caramel, 135

Red

- Radicchio salad, 144
- Tuna tartar with wasabi, 147
- Roast beef, 148
- Spaghetti a la putanesca, 151
- Thai red-curry crab claws, 152
- Seafood Paella, 154
- Blackberry and Amaretto Sherbet, 158
- Watermelon sorbet, 158
- Green tea and sesame ice cream, 159
- Banana and macadamia popsicles, 159
- Ice cream and guava sandwiches, 161
- Red fruit crumble, 162
- Strawberry clafoutis, 165

Brown

- Pecan pie, 174
- Crèpes in cajeta and tequila, 176
- Chocolate and dried fruit soufflé, 179
- Apple, date and port cake, 180
- Mushroom and parsley soup, 183
- Chicken kebabs, 186
- Beef tataki and mango skewers, 186
- Barbecued pork ribs, 187
- Sesame and mustard lamb chops, 187
- Steak al expresso, 189
- Mussels with saffron, 190
- Flamenco artichokes, 193
- Baba ghanoush, 194
- Creamy orange pâté, 197
- Honeyed turkey with cinnamon, 199

blanco

weiss

branco

white

blanc

bianco

bianco
blanc
white

blanco
weiss
branco

It is important to strain the grapefruit and to discard all of the juice. If this is not done, the taste of the vinaigrette, and the final result of the salad, may be spoiled.

Thai grapefruit and vermicelli salad

4 servings

100 grams/3 oz vermicelli
2 pink grapefruits
2 1/2 tablespoons fish sauce
6 tablespoons lemon juice
1 1/2 tablespoons rice wine vinegar
2 tablespoons dark brown sugar
1 red, fresh chili pepper, chopped and seeded
3 tablespoons roasted almonds, peeled and chopped
3 tablespoons roasted peanuts, chopped
3 tablespoons grated coconut, lightly toasted
1 cup fresh spearmint leaves, broken in pieces
2 cups assorted Asian lettuces

Cook the vermicelli in boiling water for 2 minutes.
Drain and lightly cut with scissors. Reserve.
Peel and separate grapefruit into segments. Remove the white membranes that cover them.
Let them strain well in a colander.
Mix the fish sauce, lemon juice, vinegar and sugar in a bowl until the sugar dissolves.
Add the chili pepper to sauce and reserve.
Add the vermicelli to the bowl containing the sauce and mix with a fork to loosen the strands.
Add the almonds, peanuts, coconut and spearmint.
To serve, make a bed out of the lettuces on a serving dish.
Place the grapefruit segments and vermicelli mixture on top of it.
Serve at once.

It is a good idea to divide the mixture of cornstarch and flour into two parts and use one after the other. This prevents the whole mixture from filling with lumps which, if they stick to the squid, will spoil their appearance and taste. Nor is it advisable to fry many rings at the same time because this will lower the temperature of the oil and the rings will become soggy.

Squid rings with minted lime sauce

6 servings

500 grams/17 oz clean squid rings
1 cup milk
2 tablespoons lemon juice
1 cup cornstarch
1 cup of all-purpose flour, sifted
2 teaspoons salt
1/2 teaspoon chili powder
1 teaspoon sugar
3 egg whites
Sunflower oil for frying
Lime, mint and sesame sauce, *see appendix*

Place the squid rings in a bowl, cover them with milk and lemon juice and refrigerate them for 20 minutes.
In another bowl, sift the cornstarch with the flour. Add salt, chili powder and sugar and mix well.
In a separate bowl, lightly beat the egg whites with a fork until they become foamy.
Heat the oil to 350 °F/180 °C.
Strain the squids and dry them with paper towels.
Dip them, one by one, into the egg white mixture and then in the cornstarch mixture, shaking them to eliminate any excess.
Fry them in batches in the hot oil until they are crispy and lightly golden.
Remove, and drain on paper towels. Sprinkle with salt.
Serve with lime, mint and sesame sauce.

Risotto is, in general, a main course that is not prepared for large numbers. This one is especially suitable to accompany fish and seafood.

Lemongrass risotto

4 servings

1 tablespoon olive oil
1 tablespoon onion, grated
1 $^{1/2}$ cups chicken or vegetable stock
1 $^{1/2}$ cups coconut milk, *see appendix*
2 stalks fresh lemongrass, chopped into big pieces
1 cup arborio rice
Salt and pepper

In a heavy-based saucepan, heat the oil on low heat. Add the onion and a pinch of salt.
Cook and stir until onion is tender, without letting it brown. Meanwhile, in a separate pot, boil the stock with 1 $^{1/2}$ cups of water, the coconut milk and the lemongrass.
Reduce the heat, keeping the mixture at a simmer during the cooking of the risotto.
Place the rice, without washing it, in the saucepan with the onion and stir well.
Add one ladleful of the stock mixture, taking care to avoid the lemongrass. Cook and stir over a medium heat until it is nearly dry.
Add another bit of the stock and continue to cook in the same way until the rice is *al dente*.
Season with salt and pepper, to taste.
Serve at once.

Despite a widespread belief to the contrary, bread dough does not have to be near heat to activate the yeast. A process of slow fermentation, far from heat, will ensure a better result.

Easy bread rolls

6 rolls

1 tablespoon sugar
1 tablespoon dry active yeast
2 cups all-purpose flour, sifted
1 teaspoon salt
50 grams/2 oz butter, room temperature
Vegetable oil

In a small bowl dissolve the sugar in 2/3 cup of lukewarm water, sprinkle the yeast on top and let stand at room temperature for 10 minutes to activate the yeast. It should bubble and foam.
On a work table or in a bowl, place the sifted flour with the salt and make a well in the center. Put the butter and the yeast mixture in it.
Rub the inside of a large glass bowl with oil.
Mix everything, kneading by hand until a soft, smooth and elastic dough is obtained.
Shape the dough into a ball and place in the bowl.
Cover with a moist tea towel and let it rise at room temperature until it doubles in volume.
Preheat the oven to 375 °F/190 °C.
Lightly rub a non-stick baking tray with oil.
Punch down the dough to its original size and divide into 6 equal portions. Make a ball with each one and place them on the baking tray at even intervals.
With a knife or scissors cut an x shape on the surface of each ball. Bake for 15 minutes or until they are golden brown.
Remove from oven and let stand.

Graibes

30 graibes

250 grams/8 oz clarified butter, *see appendix*
3 cups all-purpose flour, sifted
125 grams/4 oz confectioner's sugar
15 almonds, peeled and cut lengthwise
Sugar for sprinkling

Mix the butter with the flour and sugar.
Knead by hand for 1/2 hour and let stand in the refrigerator for an hour so that dough hardens and can be shaped.
Preheat the oven to 300 °F/150 °C.
Grease and flour a baking tray.
Form 6 cm/2.5 in-long ovals with the dough.
Place 1/2 almond in the center of each shortbread and arrange on the baking tray.
Bake for 20 minutes.
Remove from oven and sprinkle with granulated sugar.

Savory biscuits

26 biscuits

250 grams/8 oz butter, room temperature
375 grams/12 oz all-purpose flour, sifted
1 1/4 teaspoons salt
10 almonds, peeled and cut lengthwise

Preheat the oven to 350 °F/180 °C.
Grease and flour a baking tray.
Cream the butter with the flour and salt, to form a uniform ball of dough.
Roll out the dough with a rolling pin on a flat surface, coat with flour and cut out 6 cm/2.5 in-diameter circles. Place the circles on the baking tray at regular intervals.
Decorate with a small slice of almond in the middle.
Bake for 15 minutes or until golden brown.
Remove from oven and let cool on the tray.

Alfajores

16 cookies

150 grams/5 oz butter, room temperature
1/3 cup confectioner's sugar
1/2 teaspoon vanilla
1 cup all-purpose flour, sifted
1 cup cornstarch
3/4 cup *dulce de leche, see appendix*
3/4 cup grated coconut
Confectioner's sugar, for sprinkling

Preheat the oven to 350 °F/180 °C.
Grease and flour a baking tray.
Cream the butter with the sugar and vanilla.
Little by little, add the sifted flour with the cornstarch, mixing until it forms a soft dough.
Roll out the dough with a rolling pin on a flat floured surface until it is even and very thin, and cut out 5 cm/2 inch circles.
Arrange on the baking tray.
Bake for 20 minutes or until golden brown.
Remove from the oven and let cool.
Spread the *dulce de leche* on half of the cookies and cover with the other half. Roll the edges over the grated coconut until it adheres well and sprinkle with confectioner's sugar.

Lemon marmalade sandwich biscuits

26 biscuits

250 grams/8 oz butter, room temperature
1/4 cup sugar
1 egg
1 teaspoon vanilla essence
3 cups all-purpose flour, sifted
Lemon marmalade for filling, *see appendix*
Confectioner's sugar, for sprinkling

Preheat the oven to 350 °F/180 °C.
Grease and flour a baking tray.
Cream the butter with the sugar.
Add the egg, vanilla and flour.
Knead until it forms a soft smooth ball of dough.
Divide into two equal halves.
Roll out one half of dough with a rolling pin on a flat floured surface until it is even and thin, and cut out 5 cm/2 inch circles. Arrange on the baking tray.
Repeat procedure with the other half of the dough but as soon as the circles are cut out, open a hole in the middle of each one with a smaller cutter in order to form rings.
Bake all of the circles for 12 minutes or until golden brown.
Remove from oven and let cool.
To fill, use the whole biscuits as the base, and spread lemon marmalade on them. Sprinkle rings with confectioner's sugar and cover the marmalade rounds with them.

In almost all Latin American countries, this is a typical Christmas dish.
You must be careful to add the sugar when the rice is al dente,
or it will not be tender enough.

Rice pudding

10 servings

125 grams/4 oz rice
9 cups whole milk
1 1/2 cups sugar
3 sticks cinnamon
1 egg yolk, beaten

Soak the rice in water for two days beforehand.
Heat the milk, without boiling, for 5 minutes and add the washed and strained rice.
Cook over high heat for 18 minutes or until it is *al dente*.
Add the sugar and cook, stirring occasionally, over medium heat, for 45 minutes or until it begins to thicken.
Put the cinnamon in and stir, constantly scraping the bottom, for 3 minutes.
Remove from heat and let stand for 10 minutes.
Add the beaten yolk and mix well.
Pour into the serving bowl.
Sprinkle with cinnamon and serve cold.

Ideal to accompany thick, hot chocolate. In the best Spanish style, a good churro should have three identifiable textures – a sugar coating, a crunchy exterior and a chewy inside. The key to achieving it is the temperature of the oil.

Sugared churros

20 to 25 churros

2 teaspoons sunflower oil
1/4 teaspoon salt
1 cup all-purpose flour, sifted
Abundant oil for deep frying
Sugar for sprinkling

Boil 1 cup of water with the oil and salt.
Add the flour all at once and stir vigorously with a wooden spoon until a smooth ball of dough is obtained.
Remove from the heat and let stand.
Heat the oil until it reaches a temperature of 350 °F/180 °C.
Put the *churro* mixture into a pastry bag with a fluted tip.
Pipe out 10 cm/4 in-long strips, letting them fall into the hot oil and cooking them until they are golden brown.
Take out with a slotted spoon and drain on paper towels to eliminate excess oil.
Generously sprinkle with sugar, and serve immediately.

Delicately smooth and aromatic, this cocktail is an ideal aperitif for a dinner with a Thai flavor.

Lychee Cocktail

6 cups

1 big can, 565 grams/19 oz lychees in syrup
1/2 cup lychee syrup
1/4 cup coconut milk, *see appendix*
1 cup of crushed ice
1/2 to 3/4 cup Triple sec

Open the can and remove 6 whole lychees, put aside.
Blend rest of ingredientes until the ice acquires the consistency of a frappé.
Serve in chilled cups and decorate with the lychees that were put aside.

This dish is inspired by an ancient Lebanese tradition which maintains that white dishes are propitious symbols and represent good luck on important or festive occasions, like New Year's Eve, baptisms, weddings, or any joyous event.

Lebanese cream with mangosteens

6 servings

3 cups whole milk
7 tablespoons sugar
2 teaspoons orange blossom extract
2 teaspoons essence of roses
5 tablespoons cornstarch
1 1/2 cups nuts and dried fruits of your choosing:
pistachios, almonds, pine nuts, apricots, dates, etc.
4 mangosteens

Pour 2 cups of the milk into a large saucepan, add the sugar and the essences and bring to boil.
Dissolve the cornstarch in the rest of the milk and add to the hot mixture, stirring with a wooden spoon.
Cook over medium heat for 5 minutes or until thickened.
Remove from the heat and let cool for 10 minutes, uncovered.
Fill a 3-cup glass serving bowl or 6 individual cups with 1/2 cup capacity. Refrigerate for a minimum of 6 hours.
Sprinkle the nuts and dried fruits on top to serve and put a peeled mangosteen in the center.

The original Pavlova dessert, made up of only meringue and ice cream, was created in Perth, Australia, as a tribute to the great Russian ballet dancer Anna Pavolva during her visit to that country in the 1930s and it is meant to be as light and ethereal as her dancing.

Pavlova with coconut ice cream and lime

8 servings

6 egg whites
1/2 teaspoon cream of tartar
1 pinch salt
1 1/4 cups sugar
1 tablespoon cornstarch
2 teaspoons lime juice
3 tablespoons grated coconut

Lime Syrup
1/3 cup sugar
2 tablespoons lime juice
2 tablespoons grated lime zest

Coconut ice cream, for serving, *see appendix*

Preheat the oven to 450 °F/220 °C. Line a baking tray with wax paper.
Whisk the egg whites with cream of tartar and salt until they are frothy.
Gradually add the sugar, whisking until a thick meringue is obtained.
Carefully fold in the cornstarch, lime juice and grated coconut.
To make each "bowl" of meringue, fill a pastry bag with the mixture and form a circular base, with a 7 cm/3 in-diameter and a thickness of 1 cm/0.5 in, by piping the meringue in a rising spiral, leaving a hole in the center, until it reaches a height of 4 to 5 cm/2 in.
Lower the temperature of the oven to 250 °F/125 °C.
Bake for 50 minutes or until the meringue becomes firm, but not browned.
Remove from oven and let cool.
Meanwhile, to make the lime syrup, boil 1 cup of water with the sugar and lime juice until a syrup is formed.
Let it cool and add the lime zest.
Serve the meringue cold with the coconut ice cream in the center. Pour lime syrup on top.

Its name derived from the English pound-cake, the popular Colombian ponqué may be impregnated with different aromas – cinnamon, vanilla, lemon, orange or others – or sliced and filled with dulce de leche, marmalades, jellies and sweets.

Old-fashioned pound-cake

12 slices

250 grams/8 oz butter, room temperature
1 cup sugar
8 eggs
2 cups all-purpose flour, sifted
1 1/2 teaspoons baking powder
2 tablespoons milk
1/4 cup fresh orange juice
Confectioner's sugar, for sprinkling

Place the rack in the center of the oven.
Preheat the oven to 350 °F/180 °C.
Grease and flour a 30 cm/12 in-diameter cake mold.
Cream the butter with the sugar by hand.
Combine sifted flour and baking powder and slowly incorporate, alternating a small amount of the dry ingredients with the eggs.
Finally, incorporate the milk and orange juice.
Although the dough may seem curdled at this point, it will become smooth in the end.
Pour the mixture into the mold.
Bake for 1 hour or until the surface is browned and a skewer inserted in the center comes out clean.
Remove from oven and let cool.
Unmold and sprinkle with confectioner's sugar.

+ white…

Cardamom marshmallows

Insert skewers in the marshmallows and lightly brush with water. Sprinkle with a mixture of sugar and ground cardamom. This is a delicious adornment for hot chocolate.

Origami

With a bit of imagination and a delicate hand, the paper wrappers of disposable Chinese chopsticks can be folded into an original and practical chopstick stand.

Scented ice cubes

Fill an ice tray with water to half-way level. Add aromatic ingredients – ginger, rose petals, grated citrus zest, herbs or others – and then top up. Immediately place in freezer compartment.

A sweet-smelling refresher

On hot days, surprise your guests with cool refreshing face towels, moistened beforehand in water scented with rose or jasmine petals, which are then wrung out, rolled up and placed in the refrigerator until the arrival of your guests.

Quail eggs with anchovy and caper sauce

Mix 1/2 cup of sour cream, 6 fillets of crushed anchovies, 1 crushed garlic clove, 1 tablespoon of Dijon mustard, 1 tablespoon of chopped capers, 1 tablespoon of shredded parsley and salt and pepper to taste. Use this sauce to accompany quail eggs.

Truffle balls

Add a personal and exotic touch to the delight of truffles by putting them in a microwave oven for 3 to 5 seconds and then sprinkling them with a bit of grated coconut, curry, cinnamon powder, grated orange zest or any other seasoning you like.

Floral water

So that your guests may clean their fingers when you serve seafood, place traditional finger bowls on the table, adorned and scented with slices of lemon and a few flowers.

Flavored salt crystals

Give a touch of flavor to sea salt by adding lemons or herbs, to taste. Store it in an airtight glass container for 15 days before using to season meat or fish.

green

vert

verde

grün

grün

verde

vert

green

If you don't have time to prepare the Brie-cheese rolls, you can make croutons out of toasted bread with walnut oil and broiled cheese of your choice.

Green salad with walnuts and toasted Brie cheese

4 servings

4 sheets filo pastry
100 grams/3 oz clarified butter, *see appendix*
160 grams/5 oz Brie cheese
4 cups different lettuces, torn in pieces
1/3 cup coarsely chopped walnuts
Dijon vinaigrette, *see appendix*

Preheat the oven to broil, at 450 °F/220 °C and place an empty baking tray to heat.
Cut the Brie cheese into 8 equal portions. Separate 1 sheet of filo and quickly brush clarified butter on it. Cover with another sheet and brush again.
Cut the sheets into four equal rectangles. Keep the rest of the dough covered with a damp towel to prevent it from drying. Place 1 rectangle on a flat surface, with one edge towards you, so that it appears that you have a diamons shape in front of you.
Put one of the portions of cheese a few centimeters from the closest point of the diamond and fold dough over the cheese until it is covered. Immediately fold the side edges of the rectangle over the cheese as well and roll over until you reach the other edge.
Brush butter over the whole of the exterior.
Repeat with the remaining ingredients until 8 rolls are formed. Bake for 5 minutes, placing them directly on the hot baking tray and turning over so that they are uniformly browned. Remove from the oven.
Mix the lettuces with the walnuts and drizzle with the vinaigrette. Put the little hot Brie-cheese rolls on top and serve at once.

You may make the Brie rolls beforehand and keep them in the refrigerator until baking time.

It is not a good idea to marinate fish in lime juice for more than an hour. If left for a longer time, the lime tends to shed a tannin that affects the freshness of the ceviche and spoils its flavor.

Fish ceviche with coconut milk

6 servings

1/2 cup coconut milk, *see appendix*
1 tablespoon green chili pepper, seeded and finely chopped
500 grams/17 oz firm white fish, thinly sliced
1/2 cup fresh lemon juice
1 tablespoon fish sauce
1 cup celery, peeled and finely chopped
2 1/2 tablespoons fresh coriander leaves, chopped
Salt and pepper
3 large avocados, to serve

Heat the coconut milk with the chili pepper for 5 minutes and let it cool. (If you want a spicier preparation, infuse the milk for a longer time.)
In a medium glass bowl, combine the now cold coconut milk with the fish, the lemon and the fish sauce.
Cover and let stand in the refrigerator for 45 minutes.
Remove from the refrigerator, add the celery and coriander and season with salt and pepper to taste.
To serve, cut the avocados in half, lengthwise, and fill with the ceviche.

Although prawns defrosted in sea salt preserve much of their original taste, when you prepare these croquettes it is advisable to first fry a small portion of the mixture, so that you can sample the result and adjust its seasonings if necessary.

Mediterranean-style prawn croquettes

14 croquettes

500 grams/17 oz raw prawns
1 small red onion, finely chopped
1/3 cup Italian parsley, chopped
1/2 cup fresh spearmint leaves, chopped
1/4 teaspoon cinnamon powder
1/4 teaspoon sumac
1 pinch Cayenne pepper, ground
1 pinch chili powder
3/4 cup all-purpose flour, sifted
1/4 cup beer
1 tablespoon grated lemon zest
Olive oil for frying
Salt
Lime wedges, hummus or home-made mayonnaise with added chili oil, to serve (optional), *see appendix*

Peel and clean prawns and chop well. Strain.
If you use frozen prawns, defrost them beforehand in water with sea salt. (1 cup of sea salt to 1 gallon water)
Put in a non-metallic bowl, add the onion, parsley, spearmint and spices.
Add in the flour, mixed beforehand with 3/4 cup of water and the beer. Stir until well blended.
Cover with plastic wrap and refrigerate for at least 2 hours.
Fill a frying pan with oil to a level of 2 cm/1 in and heat well.
Take the mixture out of the refrigerator and add the lemon zest.
Pour a big spoonful of the batter into the hot oil and slightly flatten it with a metal spatula. Let each side brown for about 2 minutes, remove and drain on paper towels to eliminate excess oil.
You may fry several croquettes at the same time, but take care that they do not stick to one another.
Sprinkle with salt to taste and serve at once.
You may accompany them with lime wedges, hummus or home-made mayonnaise with chili oil.

This dish may be eaten cold or hot. It works just as well with long or short pastas and is perfect with grilled or barbecued meat.

Fresh pasta with coriander

6 servings

500 grams/17 oz spaghetti or pasta of your choosing
3 egg yolks
3/4 cup fresh coriander leaves
2 teaspoons Dijon mustard
3/4 cup olive oil
Salt and pepper

Cook the spaghetti *al dente* in abundant water with salt and a bit of oil.
Meanwhile, place the egg yolks, coriander and mustard in a blender and process until well mixed.
With the blender still running, add the oil in a thin stream until fully incorporated.
Finally, add 1/4 cup lukewarm water and season with salt and pepper to taste.
Strain the pasta and let stand until it reaches the desired serving temperature.
Mix with the sauce and decorate with coriander leaves, if you wish.

Boconccini coated with fines herbes

10 cheese balls

2 tablespoons extra virgin olive oil
1 1/2 tablespoons fresh basil leaves, finely chopped
1 1/2 tablespoons fresh chives, finely chopped
1 1/2 tablespoons fresh spearmint leaves, finely chopped
1 1/2 tablespoons fresh Italian parsley, finely chopped
Extra virgin olive oil, for serving
Salt and ground black pepper

Brush the cheese balls with oil
Mix all the herbs in a bowl.
Roll the cheese balls in the herb mixture until they are well coated.
Serve in a dish with olive oil, salt and ground black pepper.
A variant of this recipe are the "boconccini à la tapenade", prepared and served in a similar way, except that the cheeses are rolled in a mixture of 2 tablespoons of fresh chopped parsley, 1 tablespoon of chopped anchovy fillets, 1 tablespoon of chopped green olives, 1 tablespoon of chopped capers and 1/2 tablespoon of lime juice.

Vine leaf cous-cous rolls

16 rolls

1/2 cup chicken stock
1/4 cup couscous
1 big Roma tomato, peeled, seeded and diced
2 tablespoons Italian parsley, chopped
1 1/2 tablespoons lime juice
1/2 tablespoon extra virgin olive oil
1/3 cup feta cheese, crumbled into small pieces
1 tablespoon sour cream
1/2 teaspoon sumac
Salt and Szechuan pepper, to taste
16 to 20 grapevine leaves, in brine

Boil the stock. Add the couscous, stir and cook for 2 minutes or until the liquid evaporates.
Cover and remove. Let stand for 10 minutes.
Fluff up the couscous with a fork and transfer to a bowl.
Incorporate the other ingredients and stir.
Strain the grapevine leaves and arrange on a work table with the smooth part of the leaves on the underside.
Cut off stems.
Depending on the size of the leaf, put a bit of couscous, shaped into a small roll, into the lower part.
Cover this roll with the sides of the leaf and firmly roll couscous inside leaf until it reaches the upper edge.
Keep refrigerated and covered with damped paper towels until ready to serve.

Cucumber rolls with curried chicken

18 rolls

375 grams/13 oz chicken breast, deboned and skinned
1/2 cup chicken stock
1 tablespoon sour cream
1/3 cup light home-made mayonnaise, see *appendix*
1 tablespoon Indian curry powder
1 tablespoon lime juice
Salt and pepper
1/3 cup celery, peeled and finely chopped
1/3 cup raisins
2 cucumbers, washed
1 tablespoon fresh coriander leaves, chopped

Cut the breast into small cubes and cook in 1/2 cup of water and the stock. Stir for 5 minutes or until it is cooked. Take it out, strain and put in a bowl. Add the sour cream, the mayonnaise mixed with the curry and lime juice and season with salt and pepper to taste. Stir in the chopped celery, raisins and coriander.
With a mandoline, cut the outer part of the cucumbers lengthwise into slices.
Discard the seeds.
To make the rolls, wrap a slice of cucumber around two fingers to form a cylinder.
Insert a small piece of bent cucumber into one end of the cylinder to form the base and prevent the filling from spilling out. Arrange on the serving dish and fill with the chicken mixture.

Yucatan plantain chips with guacamole

8 servings

Sunflower oil for frying
2 green plantains, peeled and cut into 1 cm/0.5 in-thick slices
1 large, ripe avocado
2 tablespoons sour cream
1 $^{1/2}$ tablespoons lime juice
4 tablespoons fresh coriander leaves, chopped
4 ripe tomatoes, peeled, seeded and chopped
1 small onion, finely chopped
1 Jalapeño chili pepper, chopped and seeded
Salt and pepper

Heat oil in a deep frying pan. Fry the plantain slices for 2 minutes. Take out and drain on paper towels. Flatten the fried slices with a kitchen hammer or small board. Return to the oil for another 2 minutes or until they become brown and crisp. Take out, drain on paper towels and sprinkle with salt. Mash the avocado with a fork or in a food processor. Add the sour cream, lime juice, half of the coriander and process until it becomes smooth. Season with salt and pepper to taste. Spread the guacamole on half the chips, cover with the other half and top with some more guacamole and the tomato, onion, remaining coriander and the Jalapeño.

If you don't have a wire fish basket, always wait until the fish is well marked by the grill before turning it over. If you don't, there is a danger that it will fall apart.

Green Thai fish kebabs

8 servings

400 grams/13 oz firm white fish, either grouper, bass or swordfish
1 tablespoon sunflower oil
3 tablespoons green curry paste, *see appendix*
1/2 cup coconut milk, see *appendix*
8 small wooden skewers
8 round slices of ripe pineapple, peeled, grilled and cut into squares
24 leaves fresh basil or Thai basil
Oil for the grill
Salt

Clean the fish, removing the skin and bones.
Cut into medium-sized squares.
Heat a wok or frying pan over high heat.
Add the oil and heat until smoking.
Add the green curry paste and cook, stirring for 1 minute.
Add the coconut milk and bring to a boil until thick.
Remove from the heat and cool completely.
Add the fish to the mixture and stir well.
Transfer to a sealed plastic bag and refrigerate for 1 hour.
Soak the skewers in water.
Insert the pieces of fish on the skewers, alternating with the grilled pineapple squares and the basil leaves.
On a hot grill, rubbed with a bit of oil beforehand, cook each side for 2 minutes or until the fish is done to your liking.
As you grill, brush the skewers with some of the marinade and season with salt before serving.

If you prefer to use fresh grape leaves for this dish you need to first remove their central veins. Gently flatten them with a rolling pin, cook them in water with salt until they soften, cool them in iced water, and dry them with paper towels beforehand.

Red snapper with hummus

4 servings

2 small red snappers, cleaned and without scales
2 lemons
3 tablespoons extra virgin olive oil
8 sprigs parsley
8 to 12 grapevine leaves, fresh or in brine
1 batch hummus, *see appendix*

Preheat the oven to 400 °F/200 °C.
Diagonally score 3 to 4 cuts in each side of the fish so that the marinade penetrates well.
Rub with lemon and a little oil on all sides and season with salt and pepper.
Place the sprigs of parsley inside the belly of the fish.
Line the bottom of a baking tray with aluminum foil and brush foil with the rest of the oil.
Arrange the fish on tray and bake for 30 to 35 minutes or until the meat of the fish easily detaches from the bone.
To serve, place 2 or 3 overlapping vine leaves on a serving dish and spread a little hummus on them.
Put the fish on the bed of hummus and cover with a little more hummus and a few more vine leaves.
Repeat with the other fish and serve at once.

Be careful when you add salt to the mixture in this recipe. Both salmon and cheese have a naturally high salt content.

Asparagus and Camembert cheese quiche

8 servings

1 batch *pâte brisée*, see *appendix*
8 fresh, green asparagus
1/3 cup milk
1 cup watercress or mâche, chopped
120 grams/4 oz Camembert cheese, diced
150 grams/5 oz smoked salmon, cut in strips
3 eggs
2 egg yolks
3/4 cup heavy cream

Preheat the oven to 400 °F/200 °C.
Roll out the pastry on a flat surface dusted with flour and line a 30 cm/12 in-diameter fluted loose-bottomed tart pan. Lightly prick the pastry with a fork and line with wax paper and pastry weights or beans, and blind bake for 10 minutes. Remove the paper and weights or beans and bake for another 7 minutes, until the pastry is just about cooked but still pale.
Remove from oven and lower the temperature to 350 °F/180 °C.
Separately cook the asparagus *al dente* in boiling water with salt (the time varies in accordance with the thickness of the asparagus).
Strain and cool in iced water. Remove and dry with paper towels. Cut into medium-sized pieces and reserve.
Blanch the watercress or mâche by briefly boiling it in water. Strain and mix with the milk in a blender.
Scatter the asparagus, grated cheese and salmon strips on the dough.
In a bowl mix together the milk, eggs, yolks and cream. Season with salt and pepper to taste, and pour into the pastry shell. Bake for 30 to 35 minutes or until the filling has set.
Let cool for 5 minutes before cutting and serving.

In this recipe, which may be cooked and served in a big soufflé dish as a side dish, the broccoli can be replaced by another vegetable, in the same proportion. When using a larger dish, you must increase the cooking time until a skewer inserted into the center comes out clean.

Broccoli and Béarnaise flan

10 servings

Butter for greasing the ramekins
400 grams/13 oz peeled broccoli
4 egg yolks
2 eggs
200 grams/7 oz cream, refrigerated
Salt and pepper
Nutmeg
1 recipe of Béarnaise sauce, *see appendix*

Preheat the oven to 350 °F/180 °C.
Grease 10 individual ramekins with butter.
Cook the broccoli in water with salt until tender.
Strain. Mix in the blender with the yolks and eggs until a smooth, even purée is obtained.
Stir in the cream and season with salt, pepper and nutmeg, to taste.
Fill the ramekins with the mixture.
Place ramekins in a roasting pan lined with paper towels and fill the pan halfway with hot water. Be careful not to spill water into the ramekins.
Bake for 15 minutes, and then increase the temperature of the oven to 450 °F/220 °C and cook for another 7 minutes or until the flans are lightly browned on the surface and a skewer inserted in the center comes out clean.
Serve hot in the ramekins, bathed in the Béarnaise sauce.

+ green…

+ than color

Flowers, the universal language of love and admiration, complement the delights of good food. On festive occasions in Thailand, every woman guest receives an orchid at the end of the meal, a special gift that makes the dinner even more memorable.

+ than taste

The virtues of some foods go beyond their nutritional value or taste. A little iced water containing cucumber slices, celery stalks and mint leaves is an ideal refresher for the body and skin after a long walk or a fatiguing session at the gym.

String beans with cashew nuts

Boil 200 grams/7 oz of string beans for 4 minutes and cool in iced water. Strain and sauté in 1 tablespoon of olive oil, 1 teaspoon of sesame oil, 1/4 teaspoon of chili flakes and 3 tablespoons of toasted, chopped cashew nuts. Season with salt and serve hot.

Pasta with wasabi

To give a pleasant aroma to pasta which accompanies tuna, seafood or grilled meats, mix butter with wasabi paste and sprinkle the dish with thin juliennes of nori, the popular Japanese seaweed.

Pear frappé with mint

To make a quick pear and mint "smoothie", wash two pears, remove cores and seeds, and mix in a blender with 1/2 cup water, 1/2 cup mint leaves, 3 tablespoons of lime juice and sugar to taste. Serve at once

Basil-scented mashed potatoes

Instead of using ordinary milk for mashed potatoes, surprise your guests by infusing the milk with basil or other herbs you like.

Gauzy lemon slices

Serve fish, seafood or other dishes with a sliced lemon or lime wrapped in gauze or tulle. With this simple detail, the seeds will not fall into the food, when the lemon is squeezed.

Scented skewers

To add a special aroma to chicken, fish or seafood kebabs, use natural skewers, such as lemongrass stalks or small lemon tree branches, instead of pointed wooden sticks.

giallo

amarillo

yellow

jaune

gelb

amarelo

giallo

amarillo

yellow

jaune

gelb

amarelo

Inspired by traditional Philippine cuisine, this dish looks especially impressive when you serve it in half a coconut. You can split the coconut with a good home hacksaw or a small power saw.

Ilo-Ilo clams

4 servings

1 1/2 tablespoons olive oil
8 cm fresh ginger, grated
1 tablespoon onion, chopped
1 garlic clove, crushed
1/2 cup dry white wine
2 1/2 cups chicken or fish stock
1 kilo/2.2 lbs. clams in the shell
1 1/2 tablespoons butter
1 teaspoon oil
400 grams/13 oz squash, cut into squares
1 cup coconut milk, *see appendix*
1 red chili pepper, halved and seeded
2 tablespoons fresh coriander leaves, chopped
Salt and pepper

If you use fresh clams, discard any half-opened ones which do not close again when tapped against a table.
Heat the oil in a pot and lightly cook the ginger, onion and garlic for a few minutes.
Add the wine and 1/2 cup of the stock.
When it boils, add the clams, cover and cook for 5 minutes.
Lower the heat and remove the clams with a slotted spoon.
Discard any clams which did not open, during the cooking process.
Separately, melt the butter with the oil.
Lightly fry the squash until it becomes soft and lightly browned.
Add to the first pot and put in the rest of the stock, the coconut milk and the chili.
Boil for 5 to 10 minutes, depending on how spicy you wish and remove the chili.
Add the clams and the coriander, and season with salt and pepper, to taste.
Serve at once.

This recipe, like most Indian dishes, stands up very well to freezing, if you follow the correct steps: slightly undercook, cool to room temperature, put in the refrigerator and, finally, in the freezer. To defrost, you must follow the reverse sequence.

Hindustan-style chicken

4 servings

600 grams/20 oz chicken breast, skinned and deboned
1 tablespoon oil
1 tablespoon butter
1 large red onion, thinly sliced
1 garlic clove, crushed
1 tablespoon curry powder
1 1/2 tablespoons coriander seeds, ground
5 cm/2 in ginger, grated
3/4 teaspoon chili powder
2 cloves
1 large ripe tomato, peeled, seeded and chopped
1/4 teaspoon ground cardamom
3/4 teaspoon whole cumin seeds, ground in a mortar
3/4 teaspoon turmeric
2 medium-sized potatoes, precooked in water with salt and then diced
1/2 cup natural yogurt
Salt to taste

Dice the chicken.
Heat the oil and the butter in a pot or a deep frying pan.
Cook the onion and the garlic over medium heat until the onion is soft and translucent.
Add the curry, coriander seeds, ginger and chili, and stir.
Add 1/2 cup hot water and bring to a boil.
Add chicken, cloves, tomato, cardamom, cumin, turmeric and precooked potatoes.
Let boil for two minutes. Remove the cloves. Add the yogurt and cook for another 10 minutes, stirring occasionally.
Season with salt to taste.
Serve with white Basmati or jasmine rice.

Although the amounts of penicillin found in the magnificent blue cheeses made from cow's or goat's milk that have blue-green veins of mold, like Roquefort, Stilton or Gorgonzola, does not seem to affect those who have allergies to tpenicillin, it is advisable to confirm this before trying this dish.

Creamy carrot and blue cheese soup

4 servings

2 tablespoons butter
1 tablespoon olive oil
2 tablespoons onion, chopped
600 grams/20 oz carrot, grated
3 cups chicken or vegetable stock
1/2 cup orange juice
3 tablespoons Italian parsley
3 tablespoons olive oil
1 cup farm bread croutons
1/4 cup cream
100 grams/3 oz blue cheese
Salt and pepper

Heat the butter with the olive oil in a big pot.
Add the onion and cook until it becomes soft and translucent.
Add the carrot and cook until tender, about 15 minutes.
Add the stock, orange juice and 2 cups of water.
Bring to a boil, lower the heat and continue to cook for 15 minutes.
Separately mix the parsley with olive oil in a blender, drizzle mixture over the croutons and brown in a hot oven or frying pan.
Pour the soup into a blender and process until smooth, put back in the pot and cook for another 5 minutes. Add the cream and blue cheese, keeping a few pieces aside to scatter on top, along with the croutons.
Season with salt and pepper to taste and serve hot.

This famous soup, a classic example of French cuisine, merits a long cooking time. The slow caramelization of the onions is the secret to obtaining an excellent result.

French onion soup

4 servings

1 tablespoon olive oil
1 1/2 tablespoons butter
4 onions, peeled and finely sliced.
1 garlic clove, crushed
2 tablespoons all-purpose flour, sifted
1 1/2 cups dry white wine
2 tablespoons port
4 cups chicken stock
1 sprig thyme
1 bay leaf
1/4 cup sherry
12 to 16 thick slices baguette
2 tablespoons olive oil
1 1/2 cups Gruyère cheese, grated
1/2 cup Edam cheese, grated

Melt the oil with the butter in a heavy-based saucepan.
Add the onion and garlic.
Cook over low heat, stirring occasionally, until the onion begins to caramelize. (This process may take about 1/2 hour.)
Add the flour and cook, stirring for 2 minutes.
Add the white wine and port and let boil until it reduces by half.
Add the stock, 1 1/2 cups of water, thyme and bay leaf.
Cook for 15 minutes.
Preheat the oven to broil at 450 °F/220 °C.
Remove the thyme and bay leaf. Add the sherry and let boil for 5 minutes.
Meanwhile, brush the bread slices with oil and toast on both sides in the oven.
Pour the soup into four ovenproof bowls, preferably ceramic ones.
Soak 3 to 4 toasted bread slices in the soup and let them float on the surface of the bowl.
Sprinkle with the cheeses and broil until melted and browned.
Serve at once.

Once the cheese dissolves, this dish keeps for awhile, without needing to be heated again. This makes it perfect for a quick, informal, easy snack.

Fonduta in farm bread

2 bread bowls

1/4 cup dry white wine
250 grams/8 oz Mozzarella cheese, grated
100 grams/3 oz Gruyère cheese, grated
100 grams/3 oz Raclette cheese, grated
50 grams/2 oz blue cheese chopped
8 tablespoons milk
1 1/2 tablespoons butter
4 egg yolks
Salt and pepper
Nutmeg
2 small, round farm breads, hollowed out and with the top removed
French bread, vegetables and fruits of your choice, for serving

Heat the wine with the cheeses over a bain marie
In a separate saucepan, heat the milk and butter. When the butter melts, take it off the heat.
Wait 1 minute and add the egg yolks to milk and butter, stirring well.
Pour over the cheese and continue cooking over the bain marie, stirring continuously with a wooden spoon until it has a thick, liquid consistency. (This may take approximately 10 minutes, because at the start the cheese tends to form a compact ball that takes time to dilute.)
Once you reach this point, season with salt, pepper and nutmeg, to taste.
Pour into the two bread bowls.
Serve at once with slices of bread, apple, mushrooms or celery.

Grated potato cakes

4 servings

250 grams/8 oz potatoes
3 tablespoons butter, at room temperature
1 teaspoon salt
Pepper, to taste

Grate the potatoes with the thickest side of the grater and combine with half of the butter, salt and pepper.
In a 20 cm non-stick frying pan, melt a bit more of the butter and add the potatoes.
Cover and cook over low heat for 10 minutes.
Increase the heat a little, let brown and sprinkle with bits of butter.
Flip the cake over and brown the other side, sprinkling with the rest of the butter.
Serve at once.

Creole potatoes

16 potatoes

16 Creole potatoes
1/2 tablespoon olive oil
Salt
1/4 Parmesan cheese

Wash the potatoes well, removing the eyes.
Put the potatoes and the olive oil in a frying pan with a lid.
Cook with the lid on, over medium heat, for 12 to 15 minutes, stirring occasionally or until they are tender and browned.
Drain on paper towels.
Season with salt and sprinkle with the Parmesan cheese.

Potato balls

30 small balls

500 grams/17 oz all-purpose potatoes
1 egg
Nutmeg, to taste
Salt and pepper
2 eggs, beaten
1 cup breadcrumbs
Sunflower oil, for frying

Cook the potatoes in water with salt until tender. Strain and mash.
Add the egg, nutmeg, salt and pepper, and mix well.
Shape into 3 cm/1 in-diameter balls.
Dip them in the beaten eggs and then roll in the breadcrumbs until they are well coated.
Refrigerate for at least 30 minutes.
Fry in hot oil until browned.
Drain on paper towels.

Golden brown potato slices

6 servings

8 potatoes
2 tablespoons butter
1 tablespoon olive oil
Salt

Wash the potatoes with their skins and cook in water with salt until tender.
Cut into thick slices.
Heat the butter and oil in a frying pan.
Add the potatoes in batches and brown on both sides.
Cover, lower the heat and cook for another 5 minutes.
Remove and drain on paper towels and season with salt.
Serve at once.

These appetizing muffins have many uses. They may be served at breakfast or at tea-time. They can also be used as rolls to accompany light soups or consommés.

Cheese muffins

24 muffins

1 cup all-purpose flour, sifted
1 teaspoon baking powder
4 eggs, separated
1 cup milk
1 teaspoon salt
1 1/2 cups Mozzarella cheese, grated
125 grams/4 oz butter, melted

Preheat the oven to 350 °F/180 °C.
Grease and flour a muffin tin.
Mix the flour with the baking powder.
Add the egg yolks, milk, and salt. Mix and then add the cheese and butter.
Beat the egg whites in a clean dry bowl until soft peaks form and fold into the batter with a spatula.
Fill the tins.
Bake for 25 minutes or until a skewer inserted in the center comes out clean.

Lightly sweet and never cloying, this dessert may be served cold or hot and is the ideal finish for an Asian-style meal with strong and spicy tastes.

Baby bananas with coconut and spearmint

4 servings

1/2 cup sugar
3/4 cup coconut milk, *see appendix*
1/2 teaspoon salt
8 baby bananas
1/3 cup fresh spearmint leaves, chopped

Put the sugar in a saucepan with 1 cup water.
Boil until it has the consistency of a syrup.
Add the coconut milk and salt and cook for another minute.
Incorporate the bananas, cut into quarters, and cook for another 2 minutes.
Finally, incorporate the spearmint leaves.
May be served warm or cold

Decorating this pie with fresh passion fruit pulp accentuates its flavor, but the pulp makes it more perishable. You can obtain the same effect by increasing the amount of passion fruit extract in the recipe to 1/2 cup.

Passion fruit and white chocolate pie

10 servings

1 batch sweet pastry, *see appendix*
2 cups milk
1/2 cup cream
3 eggs
1/2 cup sugar
3 tablespoons cornstarch
1/2 teaspoon vanilla essence
1/3 cup passion fruit extract
1/8 teaspoon salt
60 grams/2 oz white chocolate, melted
Passion fruit pulp or grated white chocolate, to decorate (optional)

Preheat the oven to 400 °F/200 °C.
Roll out the pastry to line a round 30 cm loose-bottomed fluted tart pan
Lightly prick the pastry with a fork, line with wax paper and add pastry weights or beans. Blind bake for 10 minutes.
Remove the paper and the weights and bake for another 7 minutes until the pastry is just about cooked but still pale.
Take out of the oven. Lower the temperature to 375 °F/190 °C.
To make the filling, boil the milk with the cream in a heavy-based saucepan. In a separate bowl beat the eggs with the sugar, cornstarch, vanilla, passion fruit extract and salt.
Pour the boiling milk over this mixture and stir, mixing well.
Pour back into the saucepan, stirring over low heat until the mixture thickens enough to coat the back of a wooden spoon.
Remove from the heat and add the chocolate.
Stir to combine.
Put the pan on a baking tray and carefully pour the filling into the hot pastry shell.
Bake for 25 minutes.
Remove and let stand for 2 hours.
Decorate with passion fruit pulp or grated white chocolate.

The key to this recipe is to use a well-cured frying pan. To achieve this, place a new frying pan on low heat and, using paper towels, rub the pan with oil. Let it dry and repeat every 10 minutes for an hour.

Golden crèpes

12 crèpes

130 grams/4 oz Gruyère or Edam cheese, grated
1/2 cup all-purpose flour, sifted
1/2 tablespoon salt
3 eggs
1/2 cup milk
3 tablespoons beer
Toasted bacon, butter and grated lemon zest
Maple syrup or honey, to serve

Mix the grated cheese, flour and salt in a bowl and make a well in the center.
In another bowl, mix the eggs, milk and beer and slowly pour into the well, whisking all the time to incorporate the dry ingredients until a uniform batter is formed.
Cover with plastic wrap and let stand in the refrigerator for at least 30 minutes. (You may prepare the batter the day before, storing in the same conditions.)
Heat a non-stick frying pan over medium heat and pour in enough batter to coat the bottom of the pan with a thin, even layer.
Cook for 1 minute or until set and lightly golden.
Flip over and cook the other side until lightly golden.
Remove, put on a plate, repeat with the remaining batter and serve hot, accompanied by toasted bacon, butter, grated lemon zest and maple syrup or honey.

+ yellow…

Instant orange cream

If unexpected guests arrive, fill an ordinary pound-cake with instant orange cream. To do this, mix 1 cup of water, the juice of 1 orange, 1 tablespoon of cornstarch and 1/4 cup of sugar in a blender, and cook over a low heat until it thickens.

Citrus peels in syrup

Remove the bitterness of citrus peels by scraping off the inner white membrane, cutting into strips and boiling for a few minutes in water with a pinch of baking soda. Strain and rinse. Roll peels, fasten with a toothpick and cook in a syrup made of equal amounts of water and sugar until they become tender.

Butter + taste

Soften butter at room temperature and add spices, herbs or other flavors that you like – saffron, curry, caramel, cinnamon… Give it varied shapes and freeze it for use with different dishes.

Butter + color

Serve butter in rose petals, the way they do in Indochina. To do this, wrap little rolls of butter in the petals and put them in the refrigerator for a few minutes. Remove and immediately put them on the table.

Chips surprise

Prepare novel and varied chips, salty or sweet, with green plantain, cassava, white radish, pears, apples or other foods. To do it, finely slice them and fry in very hot oil.

Spicy popcorn

Transform popcorn by sprinkling it with different flavors while it is still hot, in accordance with the occasion. Use sugar or vanilla for children's parties, and saffron, curry or other spices when served as a snack.

Mango and cardamom Margarita

Blend 2 cups of ripe mango, peeled and cut into chunks, with 1/3 cup of tequila, 2 tablespoons of Cointreau and 2 cups of crushed ice. Serve in cocktail glasses, sprinkled with crushed cardamom.

Vodka gelatin shots

To enliven a fiesta, prepare, beforehand and in individual shot glasses, some vodka jellos scented with fresh fruit juice and pieces of the same fruits. Serve very cold.

orange

naranja

arancione

alaranjado

orange

naranja

arancione

alaranjado

A product of the rich seas of Japan, where it has been consumed for 1500 years, nori seaweed is an inseparable part of the Japanese diet. Its proven nutritional value and exquisite taste have made it popular all over the world.

Crunchy salmon and nori spring rolls

8 spring rolls

3 tablespoons all-purpose flour, sifted
400 grams/13 oz fresh salmon fillet, skinned
1 tablespoon mirin
1/2 tablespoon honey
1 tablespoon rice wine vinegar
1 tablespoon soy sauce
1 tablespoon sesame seeds, toasted
2 nori sheets
8 spring roll wrappers
Oil for frying
Salt
Soy sauce and pickled ginger (optional), for serving

Mix the flour with 6 tablespoons of water and cook over low heat, stirring until a thick paste is obtained. Reserve.
Cut the salmon into 8 rectangular pieces.
In a separate bowl, mix the mirin, honey, vinegar and soy sauce. Add the salmon and marinate in the refrigerator for 15 minutes. Remove, strain and sprinkle the salmon with the sesame seeds.
Cut the sheets of nori into quarters and wrap a piece of salmon in each one.
To form the rolls, place a wrapper on a flat surface, with one end towards you. Place a piece of the wrapped salmon 5 cm from this end and fold bottom corner of wrapper over fish. Fold in left and right corners. Spread paste along edges of wrapper with your finger and roll to form a tight cylinder.
Fry the rolls in hot oil until they brown on all sides. Drain on paper towels and sprinkle with salt.
Serve with soy sauce and pickled ginger.
The marinade recipe may also serve as a dipping sauce, preparing it again so that it has a crystal-clear appearance.

To enrich the taste of steamed foods, you can infuse the water used for steaming with spices or herbs. When you cook in a multi-layer bamboo steamer, you should reverse the steamers halfway through to ensure even cooking.

Fresh shrimps with chili and orange

6 servings

12 shrimps
2 oranges
2 lemon leaves or 1 lemon peel
3/4 cup basil leaves
1 stalk lemongrass, chopped
1/4 cup olive oil
1 cup cucumber, peeled and cut into sticks
1 or 2 red chili peppers, seeded and chopped
Salt, to taste

Peel and clean the shrimps. Halve lengthwise, taking care to leave the tail attached to one of the halves. Reserve the shells. Peel the oranges and with the aid of a sharp knife, cut the flesh into segments, removing the white membrane. Reserve. Half fill a wok with water. Add the orange peel, lemon leaves, half of the basil leaves, the lemongrass and the shrimp shells. Put over high heat and let boil for 2 minutes. Arrange the shrimps in a bamboo steamer, cover, and steam over the simmering water for 5 minutes or until the shrimps are pink on both sides. Remove from the heat and let stand.
Put the shrimps in a glass bowl, drizzle with olive oil and add the orange segments, cucumber, remaining basil and the chili. Season with salt, to taste. Cover with plastic wrap and let stand in the refrigerator for at least for 30 minutes or until serving time. If you prefer a spicier flavor, you may heat the olive oil with the chili, let it stand until cool and then add to the shrimp.

Each kind of pasta is made in a different way, and because of this cooking times vary. You should follow the suggested cooking time on the package and begin to check if it is done a minute before the end of the recommended time.

Pasta with caramelized pumpkin and Gorgonzola

4 servings

500 grams/17 oz Bucattini or another pasta that you like
4 tablespoons olive oil
1 tablespoon sugar
3 cups pumpkin, peeled, seeded and cut into medium-sized squares
100 grams/3 oz Gorgonzola cheese, cubed
12 sage leaves
Salt and black pepper

Cook the Bucattini *al dente* in boiling water with salt and a little olive oil.
Meanwhile, heat half of the olive oil with the sugar until it dissolves, without letting it caramelize.
Add the pumpkin and sauté until it starts to brown, 10 minutes. Lower the heat, cover and cook for another 10 minutes or until it is tender.
Separately heat the rest of the oil with the sage. Reserve.
Strain the pasta, add the cheese and stir.
Add the pumpkin and sage oil, gently stir to combine and season with salt and pepper, to taste.
Serve hot.

This Cantonese recipe, which may also be prepared with pork or shrimp, combines two important techniques of Chinese cooking: vigorous stir-frying in a wok, with a minimum of oil, and deep frying in oil, in both cases at a very high temperature.

Sweet and sour chicken with cashews

4 servings

500 grams/17 oz chicken breast, deboned and skinned
2 egg whites
3/4 cup cornstarch
2 tablespoons oil
1 big onion, sliced
1 red capsicum, seeded and finely sliced
1 carrot, finely sliced
2/3 cup rice wine vinegar
1/3 cup ketchup
2/3 cup light brown sugar
3/4 cup cashew nuts, toasted and cut in half
Sunflower oil, for deep frying

Cut the breast into cubes.
Mix the egg whites with 1/2 cup of cornstarch and 1 tablespoon of water. Incorporate the chicken and reserve.
Heat the wok, add the oil and heat until it smokes.
Add the onion and sauté for 2 minutes.
Add the capsicum, sauté for another 2 minutes.
Add the carrot and cook, stirring for 1 minute. Incorporate the vinegar, ketchup and sugar. Lower the heat and stir until it dissolves. Boil for another 2 minutes.
Dilute the rest of the cornstarch in 1/4 cup of water and add to the mixture, stirring until it boils and thickens.
Remove and let stand.
Meanwhile, in a different pan, heat oil over a high heat. Remove the chicken squares from the egg-cornstarch mixture with a fork and fry in batches in the hot oil until they are golden brown.
Remove and drain on paper towels, add to the wok and let boil. Add the cashew nuts, stir and serve at once.

Enrich the flavor of this soup by blanching and draining basil leaves and then blending them with olive oil. Drizzle over soup.

Cream of tomato soup with herb wontons

4 servings

6 big ripe tomatoes, peeled, seeded and cut in quarters
1 tablespoon sugar
1 1/2 tablespoons brown sugar
2 tablespoons olive oil
1 big can whole peeled tomatoes
2 tablespoons butter
1 onion, grated
1 garlic clove, crushed
1/4 cup dry white wine
1 1/2 tablespoons tomato purée
2 cups chicken or vegetable stock
1/4 cup cream
8 round wonton wrappers
1 batch cheese with fines herbes, *see appendix*
Salt and pepper
Oil for frying

Place the tomato quarters on a baking tray, sprinkle with the sugars and olive oil.
Bake at 265 °F/130 °C for 15 minutes, occasionally turning and basting with the juice they shed.
Strain the canned tomatoes and add to the fresh tomatoes, being careful to reserve the liquid from the can.
Stir and bake for another 15 minutes.
Remove and lightly chop. Reserve.
Meanwhile, melt the butter in a pot. Add the onion, garlic and a pinch of salt. Cook over a medium heat until the onion becomes soft and translucent, but do not let it brown. Add the wine and let it boil for 2 minutes. Add the tomato purée and cook for another minute. Put in the reserved tomatoes, the liquid from the can, and the stock. Cook for 10 minutes and tremove from heat.
Mix half in the blender, until a smooth mixture is obtained.
Pour over the non-blended half and heat.
Add the cream and stir.
Season with salt and pepper, to taste.
To assemble the wontons, pour 1 tablespoon of the cheese and herb mixture into the center of each wrapper. Brush water on the edges, fold over to form a half moon and secure by pressing first with your fingertips and then with a fork.
Fry in very hot oil until puffed and golden brown.
Serve the soup hot, topped with the wontons. You may drizzle soup with the basil oil suggested in the "tip".

To prepare homemade sour cream, beat very cold cream in a glass bowl until it begins to thicken, then add lemon juice and salt, to taste.

Twice-baked potatoes with salmon

12 servings

6 large potatoes
1/2 cup milk
1 tablespoon butter
2 tablespoons sour cream
1/2 cup cream cheese
1/2 cup Parmesan cheese, grated
1 tablespoon dill, chopped
1 tablespoon chives, finely chopped
Salt and pepper
12 slices/160 grams/5 oz smoked salmon
Sour cream for serving

Preheat the oven to 400 °F/200 °C.
Wash the potatoes well and bake with the skins for 50 minutes or until they are tender.
Cut them in half and empty them with a spoon, taking care not to break the skins.
Mash the hot potato pulp in a saucepan, add the milk and butter, stirring with a wooden spoon over low heat until fully incorporated.
Take off the heat, add the sour cream, cheeses and herbs. Season with salt and pepper, to taste. Fill the skins with the purée and bake them again at 375 °F/190 °C for 20 minutes.
Remove from the oven, top each potato with salmon and decorate with a sprig of dill.
Serve with sour cream on the side.
If you want to serve this dish as an entrée, instead of cutting the potatoes in half cut a small hole in the top and then scoop out.

Despite the widespread belief that frozen seafood is of a lesser quality than fresh seafood, defrosting in cold water with abundant sea salt restores much of its original richness and flavor.

Prawn and crayfish bisque

6 servings

500 grams/17 oz prawns
3 1/2 tablespoons olive oil
500 grams/17 oz small crayfish
1 tablespoon butter
1 red chili pepper, seeded and cut in half
125 grams/4 oz onion, finely chopped
1 garlic clove, crushed
4 saffron threads
1 1/2 pounds ripe tomatoes, peeled and diced
1 bay leaf
1 sprig fresh thyme
1 sprig fresh oregano
1 cup dry white wine
2 cups fish stock
1 teaspoon cornstarch
1/4 cup cognac
1/4 cup cream
Salt and pepper
Cognac and cream for serving
2 tablespoons chopped Italian parsley, to serve

Peel and clean the prawns. Reserve the shells.
Cut each in half lengthways, place in a bowl and add 1 1/2 tablespoons of the olive oil and 1/4 teaspoon of ground black pepper. Keep refrigerated until ready to use.
Peel and clean the crayfish well. Reserve the shells and the heads.
Heat the rest of the oil and the butter in a pot, add the chili and cook for 10 seconds or until the oil obtains the spiciness you like. Remove the chili.
Add the onion, garlic and saffron. Cook over medium heat for 5 minutes.
Add all of the shells and heads that were reserved.
Lightly fry for 1 minute. Add the tomato, bay leaf, thyme and oregano. Season with salt and pepper and cook for 8 minutes.
Add the wine and let boil for 3 minutes.
Incorporate the stock.
Cook for 5 minutes.
Adjust salt and pepper.
Lower the heat. Let stand for a few minutes and blend the whole mixture well in a blender. Strain.
Put back on the heat. Add the cornstarch dissolved in 2 tablespoons of water. When it boils, add the crayfish and cook for 4 minutes.
Remove from the heat, let stand and process in a blender again. Do not strain.
Separately sauté the prawns for 3 minutes in the same oil in which they were seasoned and flambé with the cognac.
Put the prawns in the bowls in which they are to be served and pour the hot bisque over them. Serve topped with cream and a dash of cognac. Sprinkle with parsley.

To obtain a good tempura, you should ignore the lumps in the dough and stir as little as possible with a fork. Ensure that the water is ice cold and use very hot oil for frying.

Shrimp tempura with fines herbes butter

4 servings

12 shrimps
Oil for frying
1/3 cup cornstarch
3/4 cup all-purpose flour, sifted
1 teaspoon baking powder
1/2 teaspoon salt
1 egg
Extra flour for dusting
Salt and pepper
Fines herbes butter, *see appendix*

Peel and clean the shrimps, taking care not to remove the tails. Refrigerate until ready to use.
Heat the oil in a heavy-based saucepan. Meanwhile, mix the cornstarch, flour, baking powder and salt in a bowl.
Separately beat the egg in a measuring cup. Add iced water to egg until 1 cup is reached. Pour over the flour mixture and rapidly mix with a fork or chopsticks, without whisking too much.
The batter should stay lumpy.
Dust the shrimps with flour, pat to remove excess and season with salt and pepper. Dip in the tempura batter and deep fry in the hot oil until they brown. If you use a kitchen thermometer, the temperature of the oil should read 375 °F/190 °C.
Remove and drain on paper towels.
Serve with the melted fines herbes butter.

As well as having a special fragrance and longer grain, Basmati rice refreshes the palate and combines very well with the strong spicy flavors and pleasing aromas of the Orient.

Spicy apricot Basmati

4 servings

1 cup Basmati rice
2 tablespoons peanut oil
2 tablespoons sugar
1/2 teaspoon ground cardamom
1/2 teaspoon cinnamon powder
1 clove
1 teaspoon salt
1/2 cup dried apricots, chopped

In a bowl, soak the rice in cold water for 20 to 30 minutes.
Strain.
Heat the oil in a heavy-based pot.
Add the sugar and let it caramelize.
Add the spices. Stir for 1 minute and add the rice.
Mix the salt with 2 cups of hot water. Pour over the rice and let it boil for 2 minutes.
Lower heat, cover and cook for 12 minutes.
Remove and let stand.
Add the apricots and fluff with a fork.
Serve hot.

Tangerine mimosa

6 champagne glasses

2 tangerines
3 cups cold champagne
1 1/2 cups fresh tangerine juice

Peel the tangerines and cut the flesh into segments, removing the white membrane that covers them.
Mix the champagne with the juice.
Place the segments in the bottom of the champagne glasses.
Pour the champagne on top. Serve at once.

Hot tea with Amaretto and apricot

4 cups

2 teaspoons Earl Grey tea
4 strips orange peel
2 cinnamon sticks
2 1/2 tablespoons Amaretto
1/2 cup dried apricots, sliced

Boil 3 cups of water and pour over the tea.
Let it infuse for 3 minutes and strain.
Add the strips of orange peel, cinnamon, Amaretto and apricots. Serve hot.

Goldenberry chiller

4 glasses

3 cups *uchuva* fruit (goldenberry)
1 cup crushed ice
1 teaspoon fresh ginger, grated
1 teaspoon sugar
4 lemongrass stalks

In a blender mix 2 cups of the *uchuvas* with the ice, 1 cup of water, the ginger and sugar. Strain.
Halve the rest of the *uchuvas*. Serve in chilled glasses with the halved *uchuvas* in them. Decorate each glass with a lemongrass stalk.

White peach Sangría

6 servings

1 cup apricot juice
1/2 cup ginger ale
2 cups dry white wine
1/2 cup soda water
2 tablespoons lemon juice
2 peaches, sliced
2 oranges, peeled and cut into segments
1 pear, peeled, cored and sliced
1 grapefruit, peeled and cut into segments
1 cup fresh spearmint leaves

Mix all of the liquid ingredients, which should be very cold, in a pitcher. Add the sliced peaches and the orange, pear and grapefruit segments.
Stir and add the spearmint leaves.
Refrigerate until it is time to serve.

No Indian meal would be complete without chutneys, the famous sweet or spicy sauces that were introduced to the West in the days of the British empire. In Indian cuisine, where, unlike our own, all dishes have the same importance, chutneys accompany bread and rice. Although they may be used for meat dishes, chutneys are always vegetarian.

Apricot chutney

2 1/2 cups

2 cups dried apricots, chopped
1 tablespoon *garam masala*
1/2 cup brown sugar
1/2 cup white sugar
1 cup white vinegar
1 cup cider vinegar
1 tablespoon fresh ginger, peeled and grated
1 teaspoon salt
1 cup shredded coconut, fresh or desiccated

Mix all of the ingredients with 2 cups of water in a heavy-based saucepan and let it simmer for 30 minutes or until the liquid nearly evaporates, stirring occasionally with a wooden spoon to prevent it from sticking.
Remove from the heat and let stand. It can be stored refrigerated in an airtight container for up to 30 days.

This exotic Asian treat requires a lot of patience. If you rush its preparation, you risk spoiling it. Due to its delicate texture and surprising aroma the effort is well worth it.

Carrot halvahs

10 servings

1 tablespoon sunflower oil
100 grams/3 oz butter
500 grams/17 oz grated carrot
1 1/4 cups sugar
1/4 tablespoon ground cardamom
1 cup cream
2 tablespoons slivered almonds
Oil for the baking tray
Extra almonds, for decoration

In a wok or a big frying pan, heat the oil and the butter.
Add the carrot and cook over medium heat, constantly stirring and making sure it does not brown.
When it changes color, reduce the heat and continue to cook until the liquid evaporates. Meanwhile, make a syrup with the sugar and 1/2 cup of hot water.
Add the syrup, cardamom, cream and almonds to the carrots and stir until it forms a compact mass.
Spread over a small cold baking tray, greased with oil beforehand, and let it cool for 30 minutes.
Cover with plastic wrap and refrigerate for 3 hours.
Cut into diamonds and decorate with almonds.

This dish, which must not be unmolded before it is completely cold, is an excellent crème caramel base which may be scented with different spices, according to taste.

Orange blossom crème caramel

8 servings

Caramel
1 cup sugar
2 tablespoons corn syrup
1 teaspoon orange juice

Custard
2 cups milk
1/2 cup sugar
1 cup cream
1 cinnamon stick
2 tablespoons grated orange zest
3 eggs
2 egg yolks
1 teaspoon orange blossom extract

To make the caramel, pour 1/3 cup of water into a clean heavy-based saucepan.
Add the sugar to the center, taking care to not spill any of the sugar on the edges of the saucepan.
Add the corn syrup and orange juice.
Cook over medium heat until it dissolves and begins to caramelize.
Gently swirl the saucepan in a circular motion to ensure a uniform coloring, and continue cooking until a caramel with a deep amber color is obtained.
Remove from heat and pour into 8 individual 1/2 cup capacity ramekins. Let stand until the caramel hardens and the custard is ready to go into the ramekins.
Preheat the oven to 350 °F/180 °C.
Make the custard in a saucepan by heating the milk with half of the sugar, cream, cinnamon and grated orange zest. Bring to a boil and then remove from the heat.
Meanwhile, in a bowl, mix the rest of the sugar with the eggs and yolks.
Strain the mixture of hot milk over the egg mixture.
Gently stir to combine, making sure that it does not froth. Add the orange blossom extract and pour mixture into the caramelized ramekins.
Place ramekins in a roasting pan lined with paper towels and fill the pan halfway with hot water, being careful not to spill water into the custards.
Bake for 35 to 40 minutes, or until they are firm to the touch.
Take out and let stand at room temperature, and then chill in the refrigerator.
Remove from molds onto individual plates, drizzling with the caramel from the bottom of the mold.
The creme caramels can be wrapped in plastic and stored in the refrigerator for up to 2 days before they are removed from their original molds.

+ orange....

Honeyed grapefruit with granola

There is nothing like a breakfast of appetizing and nutritious fruit to start the day. Cut a grapefruit in half, drizzle with honey and refrigerate for 30 minutes. Sprinkle granola on top just before serving.

Chocolate-coated goldenberries

Insert a toothpick into the dried goldenberries. Dip them in melted dark chocolate and place them on wax paper to dry. The result is a delicious sweet to accompany coffee at the end of a meal.

Banana spring rolls

Roll the bananas up, Philippine-style, in spring roll wrappers. Seal them with water or beaten egg, then brush with water and sprinkle sugar over them. Fry in hot oil until golden brown and serve as a dessert, alone or with ice cream.

Puff pastry twists

Sprinkle sugar and spices – such as cinnamon, poppy seeds, grated citrus zest or nutmeg – on thin, cold sheets of puff pastry, cut into long strips. Twist and bake on a baking tray lightly sprinkled with water, in a hot oven, until they brown.

Grilled peaches with Mascarpone

Strain canned halved peaches in syrup and mark them on a hot barbecue grill. Serve with Mascarpone cheese whipped with a bit of fresh scraped vanilla bean and sugar, to taste. The ideal finish to a barbecue.

Pistachio brittle

Make a caramel with 2/3 cup of sugar and 1/2 cup of water. Spread it over a silicone baking sheet and sprinkle with coarsly chopped pistachios. Let cool and cut into pieces. Great with ice cream.

Salmon cured with fresh herbs

Sprinkle fresh salmon fillets with coriander, dill, spearmint and other fresh herbs, a little sugar and sea salt. Cover and marinate in the refrigerator for 24 hours. Remove and wash. Bake, barbecue or smoke and serve thinly sliced.

Cactus fruit lollies

Clean the cactus fruits well. Cut off the top and bottom, insert an ice cream stick in the pulp and put them in the freezer for 1 hour at the most. Remove and peel them with care. A truly refreshing fruit treat for a hot sunny day.

vermelho

rojo

red

rouge

rot

rosso

vermelho

rojo

red

rouge

rot

rosso

References to this marvelous red lettuce, common in the region of Venice, go back to ancient times, when it was mentioned by Pliny the Elder. Chronicles from the Middle Ages noted that it was a popular food in monasteries and palaces. The radicchio that we use today comes from a variety with white veins, developed in Belgium in the 19th century.

Radicchio salad

4 servings

300 grams/10 oz fresh Mozzarella cheese
4 medium-sized Roma tomatoes
1 radicchio
1/2 cup fresh basil leaves

Balsamic vinaigrette
1 tablespoon Dijon mustard
2 tablespoons balsamic vinegar
2 teaspoons lime juice
6 tablespoons extra virgin olive oil
Salt and pepper

Cut the Mozzarella cheese into slices.
Cut the tomatoes into quarters.
Separate and wash the radicchio leaves
Arrange the leaves around the bottom of a salad bowl. Add the tomatoes, Mozzarella and basil.
Serve with the vinaigrette.

To prepare the vinaigrette, dissolve the mustard in the vinegar and lime, season with salt and pepper to taste, add the oil and mix well.

The wasabi, a perennial cruciferous plant that may be terrestrial or aquatic, is the traditional spicy condiment of Japanese cuisine. As well as its excellent taste and great aroma, it has anti-coagulant properties and is a preventative against tooth decay and certain types of cancer.

Tuna tartar with wasabi mayonnaise

6 servings

400 grams/13 oz fresh tuna fillet, skinned and deboned
1 1/2 tablespoons sesame oil
1/2 tablespoon light soy sauce
1/2 cup home-made mayonnaise, *see appendix*
2 tablespoons wasabi paste
Oil, for frying
18 thin wonton wrappers
1/2 cup red capsicum, finely chopped
1/2 tablespoon black sesame seeds (optional)

Cut the tuna into small cubes (do not use a serrated knife) and put into a glass bowl.
Add the sesame oil and soy sauce. Stir well.
Incorporate the mayonnaise mixed with the wasabi paste.
Season with salt and pepper to taste and let stand in the refrigerator.
Meanwhile, heat the oil in a deep frying pan and fry the wontons until they are golden brown.
Drain on paper towels.
Add the capsicum and sesame seeds to the tuna mixture just before serving.
Build towers with alternating layers of wonton and tuna mix.
Serve at once.

To ensure that your roast meat continues to look fresh and juicy, you must let it stand before slicing. Ideally, this is done on a raised rack, so that you can turn the meat over to circulate its juices, so that it does not appear gray.

Roast beef

10 servings

8 pounds beef roast
2 tablespoons olive oil
1 tablespoon mustard
1 teaspoon Worcestershire sauce
1 teaspoon black pepper
1/2 teaspoon tarragon
1/3 cup dry sherry
Salt and pepper

Preheat the oven to 450 °F/220 °C.
Rub the meat with the oil and coat very well with the mustard, Worcestershire sauce and black pepper.
Put into the oven in a roasting pan and bake for 35 minutes or until a meat thermometer inserted in the center reads 150 °F/75 °C.
Take out of the oven and let stand for 15 minutes on a rack. Meanwhile, place the roasting pan on the stove over a medium heat. Add 1/2 cup of water and heat, stirring with a wooden spoon to deglaze.
Add the tarragon and sherry. Let boil. Season with salt and pepper, to taste, and serve with roast.
Serve with string beans cooked *al dente* in water with salt and sautéed with a bit of butter.

The key to success with this pasta is the use of very ripe tomatoes. If they are not available, canned ones are a good alternative, providing they are whole, not chopped. In the case of canned tomatoes, you have to add the juice from the can and a little more sugar.

Spaghetti a la putanesca

4 servings

2 tablespoons olive oil
1 tablespoon butter
1 red chili pepper or 1 tablespoon dry chili flakes
1 garlic clove, peeled and crushed
1 red capsicum, roasted, peeled and chopped
6 ripe tomatoes, peeled, seeded and chopped
1 pinch sugar
3 tablespoons ready-made Neapolitan sauce
1/2 tablespoon dry white wine
1 small tin/56 grams/2 oz anchovy fillets in oil, chopped
1/2 cup black olives, pitted and sliced
1 1/2 tablespoons capers, chopped
1 tablespoon fresh basil leaves, chopped
1 teaspoon fresh oregano, chopped
3 tablespoons fresh Italian parsley, chopped
500 grams/17 oz spaghetti, linguini or long pasta of your choice
Salt and pepper

Heat the oil with the butter and add the chili, seeded and cut in half. Cook until the oil reaches the degree of spiciness that you like (if you use flakes you do not have to remove them.)
Add the garlic and the capsicum and cook for two minutes.
Incorporate the tomatoes, sugar and the Neapolitan sauce.
Cook for another 6 minutes.
Add the wine and let it boil.
Add the anchovies, olives, capers, basil and oregano and cook a bit longer.
Season with salt and pepper, to taste.
Sprinkle with parsley before serving.
Pour over the pasta, cooked beforehand *al dente* in boiling water with salt and a bit of olive oil.
Cooking time varies according to the kind of pasta used.

Many people refuse to prepare shellfish because they are afraid of not knowing how to eat them properly. However, in the case of crab claws, if the limbs are cracked beforehand it will be easier to handle and extract the meat.

Thai red-curry crab claws

4 servings

2 kilos/4.4 lbs. fresh crab claws with shells
4 tablespoons sunflower oil
3 tablespoons red curry paste, *see appendix*
1 tablespoon rice wine vinegar
1 tablespoon fish sauce
2 teaspoons light soy sauce
Salt
Melted clarified butter for serving, *see appendix*

Boil the claws in water with salt for 1 minute.
Strain and refresh under cold water.
Crack the crab claws, using crab crackers or the back edge of a cleaver, to help the flavor penetrate the meat. (The meat should be white, firm and not smell of ammonia.)
Heat 1 1/2 tablespoons of the oil in a wok until it smokes.
Add half of the claws.
Cook for 5 minutes and remove.
Repeat with the same amount of oil and the rest of the claws.
Remove and reserve.
Heat the wok again with the remaining oil.
Add the red curry and lightly fry for 1 minute.
Add the rice vinegar, fish sauce and soy sauce. bring to a boil.
Incorporate the claws, stirring so that they are covered with the curry mixture.
Cook for another 3 minutes. Season with salt, to taste. Serve hot with melted clarified butter.

It is important that the shelled clams shed all of the sand they contain, so that they will taste good and be pleasant to eat. To achieve this, follow a useful "grandmother's tip": leave them for a good while in a bowl of cold water with a wooden spoon inside and stir occasionally.

Seafood paella

14 servings

Seafood broth, *see appendix*
1 teaspoon saffron threads
7 garlic cloves, peeled
8 tablespoons fresh parsley, chopped
500 grams/17 oz tiger shrimps
30 prawns
500 grams/17 oz crayfish
1 1/4 cups olive oil
Salt and pepper
250 grams/8 oz shelled clams
1 cup sunflower oil
1 red chili pepper, halved and seeded
500 grams/17 oz onion, grated
11 clean squids, cut into thick slices
300 grams/10 oz red capsicum, seeded and cut into fine juliennes
250 grams/8 oz shelled peas
300 grams/10 oz ripe tomatoes, peeled, seeded and diced
250 grams/8 oz string beans, cut into pieces
500 grams/17 oz white fish fillet (snapper, grouper or sea bass), cut into medium-sized cubes
7 cups parboiled rice
30 whole clams, soaked in water

Prepare the seafood broth before beginning the paella. Reserve two cups of this broth for the cooking of the onion. In a frying pan lightly toast the saffron threads and crush them in a mortar with 5 garlic cloves and parsley. Add a cup of hot seafood broth, mix and reserve.
Clean and peel the shrimps, prawns and crayfish. Reserve the shells. Season with 1/4 cup of olive oil and a bit of black pepper. Wash the shelled clams twice in cold water to eliminate excess salt. Drain and reserve.
Heat the rest of the olive and sunflower oil in the paella pan. Brown the 2 remaining whole garlic cloves in the oil and remove them. Add the chili and heat until the oil reaches the degree of spiciness that you like. Lightly fry the seafood shells and put them into the broth, not containing the saffron. Lightly fry the shrimps, prawns and crayfish for 2 minutes. Season with salt. Remove and reserve. Lower to medium heat and add the onion. Cook for 1 hour until it caramelizes, tossing and stopping from boiling with dashes of the reserved cold broth, to prevent it from turning bitter. Raise the heat and add the squids, capsicum and peas. Sauté for 4 minutes. Add the tomato and cook, scraping the mixture until you can see the bottom of the paella pan. Add the shelled clams, string beans and fish. Incorporate the mixture of parsley, garlic and saffron. Add the rice, without washing, and lightly fry for 3 minutes, stirring so that it becomes impregnated with the sauce.
Add 7 cups of broth and wait until it boils equally in all parts of the paella pan. As it evaporates, add another 7 cups of hot broth and cook for about 25 minutes, controlling the heat so that the paella does not stick. Scatter the whole clams on top, cover with aluminum foil, lower the heat and cook for another 15 minutes until the rice is *al dente*. Remove from heat and uncover. Add the reserved shrimps, prawns and crayfish. Cover again and let stand for some 20 minutes.

Blackberry and amaretto sherbet

3 cups

3 cups ripe blackberry purée
1 1/2 cups sugar
1 tablespoon vodka
Rose petals
Amaretto caramel, *see appendix*

Mix the blackberry purée in a blender with the sugar until it completely dissolves.
Refrigerate until it is very cold. Add the vodka.
Transfer to an ice-cream maker and churn according to the manufacturer's instructions.
(Alternatively, you may pour the mixture into a metal bowl, cover with aluminum foil and place in the freezer, whisking every half hour during freezing to break up the ice crystals and obtain a creamier texture.)
Line a baking sheet with wax paper and chill sheet in the freezer.
Arrange the rose petals on the cold sheet and spoon a little sherbet on each petal. Fold the sides of the petals around the sherbet.
Put in the freezer again until it hardens
Serve with Amaretto caramel.

Watermelon sherbet

2 cups

2 cups watermelon, in purée
3/4 cup sugar
1 1/2 tablespoons lime juice
Mint syrup, *see appendix*

Stir the watermelon purée with sugar until it dissolves. Incorporate the lime juice and refrigerate for 15 minutes. Transfer to an ice-cream maker and churn according to the manufacturer's instructions. Place the sherbet in a bowl and put it into the freezer until it acquires a firm consistency. (Alternatively, you may pour the mixture into a metal bowl, cover with aluminum foil and place in the freezer, whisking every half hour during freezing to break up the ice crystals and obtain a creamier texture.) Serve in cold cups, with mint syrup poured on top.

Green tea and sesame seed ice cream

2 cups

1 1/2 cups milk
1/2 cup sugar
1 tablespoon green tea leaves
3 egg yolks
1 cup cream
Green food coloring
1 batch sesame caramel crunch, chopped, *see appendix*
1 egg white
1 tablespoon sugar
Raspberry sauce, *see appendix*

Heat the milk in a saucepan with half of the sugar, without letting it boil. Turn off the heat and add the tea leaves. Infuse for 3 minutes. Pour over the yolks beaten with the rest of the sugar and cook, stirring over low heat until the mixture thickens enough to coat the back of a wooden spoon.
Strain into a bowl and set bowl on ice to cool. Whisk the cold cream until it thickens. Incorporate into the above mixture. Add coloring, to your liking.
Transfer to an ice-cream maker and churn according to the manufacturer's instructions.
(Alternatively, you may pour the mixture into a metal bowl, cover with aluminum foil and place in the freezer, whisking every half hour during freezing to break up the ice crystals and obtain a creamier texture.)
Meanwhile, whisk the egg white into soft peaks, incorporating the sugar little by little.
Add this meringue and the chopped sesame crunch to the ice cream before the churning is complete.
Serve with raspberry sauce on top.

Banana popsicles with macadamia nuts

4 servings

4 baby bananas
4 ice cream sticks
100 grams/3 oz white chocolate, melted
1/3 cup macadamia nuts, shelled, peeled and chopped
1/3 cup dried cranberries, chopped
1 batch blackberry sauce, *see appendix*

Peel the bananas and insert the sticks.
Melt the chocolate over a bain marie and cover the bananas with chocolate. While the chocolate is still hot, sprinkle with the chopped macadamias and cranberries.
Place on a baking tray lined with wax paper and put in the freezer to harden.
Serve cold, drizzled with blackberry sauce.

What makes this dessert appealing is its combination of hot and cold. The ice cream must be sufficiently firm before browning the toast and should be served at once.

Toasted ice cream and guava sandwiches

6 servings

12 thick slices white bread
2 cups vanilla ice cream, *see appendix*
Aluminum foil
2 eggs
1/2 cup milk
1/3 cup cream
1 teaspoon vanilla extract
1 teaspoon cinnamon powder
Butter for cooking
Sugar for sprinkling
24 guava halves poached in syrup, *see appendix*
1/2 cup maple syrup
Spearmint, for decoration

Spread vanilla ice cream on half of the bread slices and cover with the other half, forming 6 sandwiches.
Immediately wrap in aluminum foil and put in the freezer for 30 minutes until they harden.
Mix the eggs with the milk, cream, vanilla and cinnamon.
Take the sandwiches out of the freezer.
Dip them in the mixture.
Cook in a very hot frying pan with butter, until they are browned on both sides.
Sprinkle with sugar.
Serve at once, crowned with the guava halves and drizzled with maple syrup.
Decorate with spearmint.

A crumble adds a special touch to desserts. To give it that light and crumbly texture, you have to delicately sprinkle the mixture over the fruit, allowing it to gently fall and loosely cover the fruit.

Red fruit crumble

4 servings

1 1/2 cups strawberries, cut into quarters
1 1/2 cups blackberries, without stems, cut in half
1 1/2 cups raspberries
1 tablespoon Amaretto
1 1/2 tablespoons sugar
1 1/2 teaspoons grated orange zest
3/4 cup all-purpose flour, sifted
1/4 cup brown sugar
1/4 cup almonds, toasted and ground
1/2 teaspoon salt
1/4 teaspoon cinnamon powder
100 grams/3 oz butter, chilled and cubed
Whipped cream or vanilla ice cream (optional), to serve,
see appendix

Adjust rack in the center of the oven.
Preheat the oven to 375 °F/190 °C.
Place the fruits in a bowl.
Add the Amaretto, sugar and orange zest.
Let it marinate.
Separately mix the flour, sugar, almonds and salt. Add the cold butter and incorporate with your fingertips until the mixture resembles coarse bread crumbs.
Keep refrigerated until needed.
Place the fruits in the bottom of one, or several, ovenproof molds and cover with the crumbs of dough.
Bake for 20 minutes or until the surface browns.
Serve hot with whipped cream or vanilla ice cream, if you wish.

Clafoutis are normally made with fresh, whole cherries, to stop the dish from becoming red and soggy. Since strawberries are used in this case, which also bleed, the clafoutis are prepared without the fruit, which is served on top at the end.

Strawberry clafoutis

6 servings

Butter and sugar for the mold
3 eggs
4 tablespoons sugar
1/2 cup all-purpose flour, sifted
1 teaspoon vanilla extract
3/4 cup cream
1/3 cup milk
1 tablespoon butter, cut into pieces
4 cups fresh ripe strawberries, stems removed
1 1/2 tablespoons sugar
2 cubes crushed ice

Preheat the oven to 400 °F/200 °C.
Grease and sugar one or several shallow ovenproof molds.
Mix the eggs with the sugar in a bowl and incorporate the flour.
Add the vanilla, cream and milk. Stir well.
Pour into the mold.
Scatter pieces of the butter over the surface.
Bake for 35 minutes or until a skewer inserted into the center comes out clean and the surface is golden brown.
Meanwhile, cut the strawberries into quarters and put into a bowl. Sprinkle with sugar, add the ice, stir and let stand.
Serve with the strawberries on top.

+ red…

Berry-flavored vodka

Give a special flavor to vodka by using assorted berries, letting them marinate in the liquor for 1 month. If you want a sweet drink, add sugar at the end of that time and store for another 15 days.

Blackberry and coconut shake

For an exotic and delicious iced poolside refreshment, blend 2 cups of blackberries, 3/4 cup of coconut milk, 1/2 cup of vanilla ice cream, 1 cup of ice, and sugar to taste.

Blackberry jam

Boil 400 grams/13 oz of blackberries in 6 cups of water until they whiten. Strain everything into a clean saucepan, pressing to extract the pulp. Discard the seeds. Add 2 cups of sugar and the juice of 1/2 lemon. Cook until it has the consistency you like.

Fruit syrups

To prepare fruit syrups of different flavors, boil equal amounts of sugar and water, let it thicken a little, add the fruits that you like, cook for a few minutes and let stand. An ideal accompaniment for pancakes.

Beet-root chips

For a delicious and unusual snack, peel the beet-roots, finely slice them and fry in hot oil until they become crunchy.

Prosciutto and date snack

Wrap seedless dates in basil or fresh mint leaves and then roll strips of prosciutto around them and secure with toothpicks. These are an ideal appetizer to accompany red wines.

Variations of barbecue sauce

The barbecue sauce found in the appendix offers a versatile basis for variations with aromas of your choice. You can change some ingredients and heighten or reduce the degree of sweetness, spiciness or sourness.

Slow-baked tomatoes with herbs

Peel the tomatoes, cut them into quarters and remove the seeds. Bake them at 275 °F/140 °C for 40 minutes, sprinkled with olive oil, salt, sugar and herbs. Baste and turn occasionally during baking.

braun

café

brown

brun

marrom

marrone

braun

café

brown

brun

marrom

marrone

You must not skimp on the ingredients nor alter the cooking times for this delicious pecan pie. Don't worry if it feels soft when you take it out of the oven: it will reach the right consistency after it stands a while.

Pecan pie

8 servings

1 batch pastry for pecan pie, *see appendix*
100 grams/3 oz butter
1/2 cup dark brown sugar
1/4 cup light brown sugar
1/4 teaspoon salt
3 eggs
1 tablespoon vanilla extract
1/3 cup cream
3/4 cup corn syrup
1 cup pecan nuts, coarsely chopped
1 cup pecan nuts, whole

Preheat the oven to 400 °F/200 °C.
Roll out the pastry to line a round 30 cm/12 in loose-bottomed fluted tart pan.
Lightly prick the pastry with a fork and line with wax paper and pastry weights or beans. Blind bake for 15 minutes. Remove the paper and the weights and bake for another 6 minutes until the pastry is just about cooked but still pale.
Brush pastry with an egg lightly beaten with a bit of water, and bake for another 2 minutes.
Take out of the oven and lower the temperature to 300 °F/150 °C.
Melt the butter and, away from the heat, add the sugars and salt. Stir well.
Separately whisk the eggs with the vanilla and add the cream. Add to the butter and stir well.
Add the hot corn syrup and stir with a wooden spoon until the mixture is smooth and shiny. Add the chopped nuts.
Pour into the warm pie shell, scatter the whole nuts over the surface and bake for 45 minutes.
Turn off the oven, leaving the pie inside and let it cool down. Once the pie is at room temperature, remove it from the oven.
This pie may be kept at room temperature for up to 3 days.

Do not eat this pie when it is still hot from baking. If you want to serve it warm, reheat before serving.

These crèpes make a very good finish to a Mexican-style meal. The orange reduces the sweetness of the cajeta, and you should not let it boil because the sauce will curdle. The pine nuts may be replaced with other nuts, like chopped walnuts or almonds.

Crèpes in cajeta and tequila sauce

6 servings

1 batch crèpes batter, *see appendix*
3 tablespoons butter
3/4 cup *cajeta*
1/2 cup orange juice
2 tablespoons tequila
1/2 cup pine nuts, lightly toasted
Vanilla ice cream for serving (optional), *see appendix*

Heat a bit of butter in a frying pan and pour in 2 or 3 tablespoons of the crèpe batter, swirling the pan until the bottom of the pan is covered with a thin layer.
Cook for 1 minute. Flip the crèpe over with a spatula and cook for another 30 seconds or until lightly browned.
Remove and put on a plate and repeat until you use all of the batter.
Fold the crèpes in half and then fold them again, to form triangles.
Melt a tablespoon of butter in a saucepan. Add the *cajeta* and orange juice.
Heat, stirring until the cajeta melts, but without letting it boil.
Melt the rest of the butter in a frying pan.
Add the folded crèpes in a single layers. Add the tequila and flambé.
Cover with the sauce and add the pine nuts.
Serve hot, with vanilla ice cream, if you wish.

If you prepare the crèpe batter beforehand, you may add a little bit of water to it before beginning to cook the crèpes, in order to restore its original consistency.

When you melt chocolate remember that it does not tolerate high temperatures, contact with water, or any air that may be inadvertently incorporated if you if whisk it excessively.

Dark chocolate and dried fruit soufflé

8 servings

1/2 cup raisins
1/2 cup seedless dates, chopped
1/2 cup almonds or walnuts, peeled and chopped
1/2 cup port
1 tablespoon butter
Sugar to coat the mold
6 egg yolks
1/4 cup sugar
1 tablespoon all-purpose flour, sifted
1/4 cup cornstarch
2 １/4 cups whole milk
2 tablespoons chocolate liquor
1/2 cup unsweetened cocoa powder
200 grams/7 oz dark chocolate
2 tablespoons butter
10 egg whites
1/4 teaspoon cream of tartar
2 tablespoons sugar

Preheat the oven to 375 °F/190 °C.
Put the dried fruits and nuts in a saucepan and add the port.
Let it boil for 2 minutes or until the liquid evaporates.
Remove, let stand and reserve.
Grease and sugar a 7-cup capacity soufflé dish.
Whisk the yolks with half of the sugar in a bowl until they are pale and creamy.
Add the flour and cornstarch. Stir well.
In a medium-sized saucepan, put the milk with the rest of the sugar and cook over a medium heat until it boils.
Pour over the yolk mixture, whisking constantly. Transfer to a clean saucepan and cook, stirring constantly, until a thick, smooth cream is obtained. Remove from heat.
Incorporate the chocolate liquor, the cocoa and the chocolate melted with the butter beforehand in a double boiler or microwave oven.
Add the reserved dried fruits and nuts.
In a dry bowl, whisk the egg whites until they are frothy.
Add the cream of tartar and sugar, little by little.
Continue whisking until soft peaks form.
With a hand whisk incorporate 1/4 of the egg white mixture into the chocolate mixture in order to lighten it and then gently fold in the rest with a spatula. Spoon into the prepared mold. Run the tip of your thumb around the inside rim of the dish to help the soufflé rise without sticking.
Bake for approximately 30 minutes or until the soufflé rises and browns.
The inside must remain creamy.
Serve immediately.

*This sophisticated cake is ideal for special celebrations.
If you wish it to be darker, you may use brown sugar or add tincture of panela.*

Apple, date and port cake

12 servings

1/2 cup sugar
1 clove
3/4 cup port
3/4 cup prunes, seedless and chopped
1 cup dates, seedless, cut into little strips
1/2 cup almonds, peeled and chopped
2 apples, peeled and cut into medium-sized cubes
250 grams/8 oz butter, room temperature
1 1/4 cups sugar
1/4 cup grated *panela* (rock sugar or brown sugar loaf)
2 cups all-purpose flour, sifted
1 1/2 teaspoons cinnamon powder
1/4 teaspoon nutmeg, grated
1/2 teaspoon baking powder
6 eggs
1 teaspoon grated orange zest
Port and nut fudge sauce, *see appendix*

In a saucepan boil 3/4 cup of water with the sugar and clove to form a syrup.
Remove the clove. Add the port and let it boil.
Add the prunes, dates, almonds and apples.
Cook for 3 minutes. Remove from the heat and let stand.
Preheat the oven to 350 °F/180 °C.
Grease and flour a 30 cm diameter cake mold.
Cream the butter with the sugar and *panela* until fully incorporated. Little by little add the flour sifted with the cinnamon, nutmeg and baking powder, alternating with the eggs. Lastly, add the grated orange zest, dates and other marinated fruits and nuts. Pour into the mold.
Bake for 1 hour or until a skewer inserted into the center comes out clean. Let it stand and unmold.
Serve covered with the port and nut fudge.

This elegant soup, designed to be served in small cups, like a good coffee, is an extraordinary aperitif. Its original taste and texture will stimulate the appetite and delight the palate.

Mushroom and parsley capuccino-soup

6 servings

3 tablespoons butter
1 teaspoon olive oil
2 cups mushrooms, cut into quarters
2 tablespoons onion, finely chopped
2 garlic cloves, crushed
1/4 cup dry white wine
1 1/2 cups chicken stock
1 cup Italian parsley leaves
3 tablespoons cream
80 grams/3 oz butter, chilled and cubed
Salt and pepper

Melt 2 tablespoons of the butter with the oil in a saucepan over high heat.
Add the mushrooms and brown on all sides. (Do not add salt at this stage.)
Remove from the heat and reserve.
Melt the remaining butter and cook the onion and garlic over low heat until the onion becomes soft and translucent. Do not let it brown.
Add the white wine and let boil for 1 minute.
Incorporate 3/4 of the mushrooms, the stock and the parsley and cook for 15 minutes.
Add the cream. Remove from the heat and let stand for 2 minutes.
Mix the hot mixture in a blender, or with a hand mixer, adding the cold butter little by little until it is completely incorporated.
Season with salt and pepper to taste, serve in coffee cups and divide remaining mushrooms evenly among cups.

184

Chicken kebabs

10 kebabs

1 tablespoon ginger, grated
1/4 cup mirin
1/4 cup rice wine vinegar
1 1/2 tablespoons soy sauce
1/4 cup granulated dashi, dissolved in water
1500 grams/50 oz chicken breasts, cut into thin strips
5 scallions, cut into 6 cm/2.5 in pieces
10 wooden skewers
Salt and pepper

In a glass bowl put the ginger, mirin, vinegar, soy sauce and dashi.
Stir to blend the flavors well.
Add the chicken and mix well with the marinade.
Cover with plastic wrap and refrigerate for at least 1 hour.
Meanwhile, soak the skewers in water.
Remove and thread the chicken strips onto the skewers, alternating with the scallion pieces.
Cook over a hot grill or barbecue for 4 minutes on each side until the meat is browned and cooked through.
Season with salt and pepper, to taste.

Beef tataki and green mango skewers

12 skewers

500 grams/17 oz beef fillet
1 1/2 tablespoons sunflower oil
2 tablespoons spearmint, chopped
1 tablespoon black peppercorns, crushed
1 garlic clove, crushed
1 tablespoon sweet chili sauce
2 1/2 tablespoons lime juice
1 1/2 tablespoons fish sauce
12 small wooden skewers
1 green mango, peeled and cut into squares
1/3 cup spearmint

Rub the meat with oil and then press the crushed peppercorns and spearmint into it.
In a separate small bowl put the garlic, sweet chili sauce, lime and fish sauce. Stir and reserve.
Heat a frying pan without oil until it is very hot.
Add the meat and cook over high heat for 3 or 4 minutes on all sides. Remove and let stand for at least 5 minutes.
Cut meat into thin slices and insert the sticks into the beef, alternating it with the green mango and spearmint leaves.
Drizzle with the reserved sauce and serve.

Barbecued pork ribs

6 servings

1 1/2 kilos pork ribs
1/2 cup prunes, pitted
1/4 cup ketchup
1/4 cup dark brown sugar
3 tablespoons Worcestershire sauce
1 tablespoon rice wine vinegar
Hot chili sauce, to taste
Salt

Brine the pork rack in salted water with a little sugar and refrigerate overnight.
Strain and separate ribs, placing them in a glass bowl.
Hydrate the prunes in boiling water, strain and let stand.
Mix prunes in blender with remaining ingredients and 1 tablespoon of water, reserving a couple of tablespoons of this sauce.
Pour the remaining sauce over the ribs and rub until well coated.
Cover and let stand for a minimum of 30 minutes.
Cook on the barbecue for about 15 minutes, turning over until they are browned and cooked inside.
Brush the ribs with the reserved sauce during the last 2 minutes of cooking to avoid burning.
Season with salt to taste.

Sesame and mustard lamb chops

4 servings

12 lamb chops
1/2 tablespoon sesame oil
1 tablespoon Dijon mustard
Salt and pepper
1 tablespoon sesame seeds

Thoroughly rub the lamb chops with the oil and mustard.
Put in a glass bowl, cover with plastic wrap and refrigerate for 1 hour.
Cook either in a hot ungreased frying pan, or grill or barbecue, for 4 minutes on each side or until they are cooked to your liking.
Season with salt and pepper and sprinkle with the sesame seeds.
Serve at once.

One should try to overcome certain preconceived ideas about cooking meat. To obtain a better texture and juiciness, you may turn each steak over 4 times while cooking. This enables the juices to spread around evenly, and prevents the meat from becoming dry.

Steak al expresso

4 servings

4 beef steaks, (180 grams/6 oz each)
2 tablespoons sunflower oil
1 1/2 tablespoons black peppercorns, crushed
2 tablespoons ground coffee
70 grams/2 oz butter, at room temperature
50 grams/2 oz blue cheese
1 1/2 tablespoons Italian parsley, chopped
3 tablespoons butter, for cooking the meat
1 teaspoon oil
Salt
3 tablespoons whisky or cognac

Rub the beef steaks with the oil and press the previously mixed crushed peppercorns and ground coffee into them.
Cover with plastic wrap and let stand for several minutes.
Meanwhile, mash the room-temperature butter and the blue cheese with a fork and mix until soft and well combined. Stir in the parsley.
Place this mixture on a sheet of wax paper or plastic wrap and shape to form small loaf.
Refrigerate until it hardens.
As soon as it is firm, take out of the refrigerator, remove the wrapper and cut into 4 thick slices.
Heat the remaining butter and oil in a frying pan over high heat.
Add the steaks and cook for 2 to 4 minutes on each side, or to your liking.
Season with salt.
Put a piece of butter on each steak.
Add the whisky or cognac and flambé.
Remove from heat and serve at once.

There is no mystery to selecting the ingredients for this recipe: the mussels and clams themselves will show you whether they are good to eat. Shells should be tightly closed, or close quickly after a tap on the table, be intact and look glossy.

Mussels with saffron

4 servings

2 kilos/4.4 lbs. mussels in their shells
2 tablespoons butter
1 tablespoon olive oil
1 medium-sized onion, chopped
1 pinch saffron threads
1 stalk celery, peeled and chopped
1 garlic clove, peeled and crushed
1 ripe tomato, peeled, seeded and chopped
1 3/4 cups dry white wine
1 bay leaf
3/4 cup cream
Salt and pepper
3 tablespoons chopped Italian parsley
1 tablespoon chopped chives

Scrub the mussels well in cold water and remove the "beards".
Melt the butter with oil in a large pot. Add the onion and cook over low heat until it is soft and translucent. Add the saffron and cook for 1 minute. Add the celery, garlic and tomato and cook for another 2 minutes. Incorporate the wine and bay and let it boil for 2 minutes.
Add the mussels, cover and cook for 3 to 5 minutes or until they open.
With a slotted spoon, remove the mussels and place them in a serving dish. Discard those which have not opened.
Strain the sauce into a clean saucepan and let it boil for 3 minutes.
Add the cream.
Season with salt and pepper, to taste.
Incorporate the chopped herbs and pour sauce over the mussels.
Serve at once, accompanied by bread or French fries.

When you have to cook meat for a long time to tenderize it, you can save the resulting juices and use them as a base to prepare broth. To do this, let it cool, remove the layer of grease that forms on the surface and make it into ice cubes or freeze in plastic bags.

Flamenco artichokes

10 servings

100 grams/3 oz butter
8 tablespoons olive oil
1 onion, grated
4 large scallions, thinly sliced
10 ripe tomatoes, peeled and chopped
2 cups very rich meat stock
2 teaspoons ground black pepper
1/2 cup beer
10 artichokes
Salt
1 recipe Hollandaise sauce, *see appendix*

Heat the butter with the oil in a pressure cooker.
Add the onions with a pinch of salt and cook for 15 minutes or until they are soft and translucent and the oil begins to separate.
Add the tomato, stock and pepper.
Cook for 25 minutes.
Add the beer and the artichokes and cook for 5 minutes.
Incorporate 6 cups of water and 1 teaspoon of salt.
Bring to a boil.
Pressure cook for 45 minutes.
Serve with Hollandaise sauce.

To make the eggplant purée in this recipe the eggplants must be very ripe. To determine this, choose the ones with the darkest color and ensure that their bottoms slightly sink in when pressed.

Baba ghanoush

1 cup

2 large eggplants, weighing 500 grams/17 oz each
1 garlic clove, peeled
2 tablespoons of tahini paste
1 1/2 tablespoons lime juice
1 1/2 tablespoons olive oil
Salt and pepper
Extra virgin olive oil, to drizzle (optional)

Cook the eggplants in an oven preheated to broil at 500 °F/ 250 °C, or on a very hot grill, until the skin wrinkles on all sides and the eggplants are uniformly soft when you press them with a spatula (about 50 minutes in the oven or 25 minutes on the grill.)
Remove and let stand for a few minutes.
Meanwhile, boil the garlic in water for 1 minute, remove and chop.
Cut off the ends of the eggplants and halve them lengthwise. With the aid of a spoon, remove the pulp and strain in a colander over a bowl. Discard the skins.
Ten minutes later process the pulp with the rest of the ingredients until a textured purée is obtained.
Pour into a glass bowl, cover and refrigerate for 30 minutes. Serve with pita bread, drizzling a bit of extra virgin olive oil over it.

This is a creamy pâté, which should not be removed from its mold. For this reason you should prepare it from the start in the dish in which it will be served and decorate it with the cubed gelée.

Creamy orange pâté

12 servings

500 grams/17 oz chicken livers
1 cup milk
3 tablespoons Cointreau
1/4 cup dry white wine
6 tablespoons butter
1 small onion, finely chopped
1 garlic clove, crushed
1/3 cup cream
Salt and pepper
Orange gelée, for serving (optional), *see appendix*

Clean the livers, removing the veins and any dark spots they may have. Wash in cold water, dry with paper towels and cut in half.
Place in a bowl, cover with the milk and let stand in the refrigerator for 20 minutes. Strain and discard the milk. Add the Cointreau and white wine to the livers. Put back in the refrigerator and let them marinate for 2 hours. Strain and reserve the liquid. Melt half of the butter in a frying pan, leaving the other half at room temperature.
Add the onion and the garlic. Cook over low heat until the onion is soft and translucent. Add the livers. Stir occasionally and cook until they change color. Incorporate the liquid from the marinade and let boil for 2 minutes.
Remove from the heat and let stand for several minutes. Process everything in a blender or food processor until a uniform mixture is obtained. Little by little add the remaining soft butter and the cream.
Season with salt and pepper to taste.
Pour into a serving dish, smooth out the surface and refrigerate for at least 2 hours before serving.
If you wish you may serve it decorated with the cubed gelée or grated orange rind.

A traditional dish for the Christmas season, turkey is becoming a very popular meal. This recipe may be accompanied by sweet fruit sauces or compotes, such as apple, prune or rhubarb.

Honeyed turkey with cinnamon

12 servings

1 cup salt
1 cup sugar
One 6-pound turkey breast
2 tablespoons Cointreau or Grand Marnier
Salt and pepper
50 grams/2 oz butter, melted
2 tablespoons soy sauce
2 tablespoons honey
1 tablespoon cinnamon powder
1 carrot, chopped
1 stalk celery, chopped
1 small onion, chopped
1 apple, cut into cubes
1 tablespoon olive oil or butter
3 garlic cloves
3 anise stars
3 cinnamon sticks
1/4 cup dry white wine
1/4 cup chicken stock
Wine sauce for turkey (optional), *see appendix*

Put the salt and sugar in a large pot and dissolve in small amount of water. Add more water (the amount will depend on the size of your turkey breast) and submerge the turkey breast. Cover and refrigerate for 5 hours.
Preheat the oven to 450 °F/220 °C.
Drain and wash the breast well until there are no traces of salt or sugar. Dry with paper towels.
Inject the Cointreau or Grand Marnier into different parts of the breast with a syringe.
Sprinkle with sufficient salt and pepper.
Rub with a mixture of the melted butter, soy sauce and honey.
Sprinkle with the powdered cinnamon.
Lightly grease a roasting pan with oil.
Place the carrot, celery, onion and apple, sautéed beforehand in the oil or butter, at the bottom of the pan and place a rack over the vegetables.
Rest the breast on the rack. Add the whole garlic, anise stars and cinnamon sticks, placing them in bottom of roasting pan..
Pour the white wine and the stock into the bottom of the pan.
Bake for 30 minutes or until the turkey is browned.
Cover with aluminum foil and lower the temperature to 330 °F/170 °C.
Continue to cook until a thermometer inserted in the meat registers a temperature between 165 and 170 °F/80 and 85 °C, which may take another $1^{1/2}$ hours, approximately.
Remove from the oven and let stand for 20 minutes, before carving and serving.
You may serve it with the suggested wine sauce.

+ brown...

Peanut butter chili sauce

Heat 1/2 cup of crunchy peanut butter, 1/2 cup of chicken or vegetable stock, 1/2 cup of coconut milk, 2 tablespoons of lemon juice, 1 tablespoon of sweet chili sauce and 1 tablespoon of soy sauce for a couple of minutes. Good to serve with meat patties, lamb chops or chicken satays.

Caramelized brie

Heat a Brie or Camembert cheese in its box in the oven at 200 °C/400 °F for 10 minutes. Separately dissolve on the stove 1 1/2 tablespoons of dark brown sugar and 1 tablespoon of corn syrup. Pour this over the cheese, sprinkle with a little nutmeg and serve hot.

Honeyed nuts with spices

In a non-stick frying pan heat a little honey, add a mixture of nuts of your choosing and sauté them until they are well coated. Remove, place on wax paper and let them cool. Before serving, sprinkle with spices of your choice.

Cold coffee cake

In a mold intercalate 4 layers of Graham crackers or petit beurre biscuits, dipped in strong black coffee, with 3 layers of soft butter whisked with sugar and instant coffee powder. Refrigerate until it hardens. Serve cold, cut into squares and sprinkled with a little Dutch cocoa.

Dulce de leche express

For a home-made dulce de leche, cook 1 unopened can of condensed milk in a pressure cooker for 1 hour. Remove and let cool, still closed, for another hour before serving.

Cold Viennese hot chocolate

Prepare a very thick hot chocolate with equal portions of milk and water. Let it cool and generously mix with very cold vanilla Chantilly cream. To prepare the cream, see appendix.

Thai-style bicolor coffee

Prepare a strong coffee and let it cool. Separately mix a bit of condensed milk with ground cardamom. Fill a cup with ice and coffee. Gently pour a thin stream of condensed milk into the center. It will fall to the bottom without clouding the coffee.

Delightful home-made teas

Taking advantage of the wide range of teas that are sold nowadays, prepare combinations of your choice in small bags of gauze or tulle, tied with a thin cord that allows the bag to be removed when infusion is complete.

Appendix

Amaretto caramel

1/2 cup sugar
1 tablespoon corn syrup
5 tablespoons Amaretto

Put the sugar with 1/2 cup of water in a heavy-based saucepan and heat until it caramelizes. Then add to this the corn syrup and Amaretto. Heat for another 5 minutes. Take off the heat and let stand.

Barbecue sauce
Makes 2 cups

3 tablespoons onion, grated
1 tablespoon butter
2 tablespoons maple syrup
1 tablespoon honey
1/3 cup Worcestershire sauce
1 cup ketchup
5 tablespoons brown sugar
3 tablespoons cider vinegar
1 tablespoon lemon juice
1 tablespoon hot chili sauce
1 tablespoon mustard
1 tablespoon cornstarch

Cook the onion in the butter until it softens. Add the maple syrup, honey, Worcestershire sauce, ketchup, sugar, cider vinegar, lemon juice, hot chili and mustard and boil for 20 minutes, stirring occasionally. Incorporate the cornstarch dissolved in 1/2 cup of water and stir until it thickens. Strain and let stand. It may be kept for up to 2 weeks by refrigerating in an airtight container.

Béarnaise sauce
Makes 1 cup

1 tablespoon onion, finely chopped
1 tablespoon tarragon, dry
3 tablespoons vinegar or dry white wine
2 egg yolks
125 grams/4 oz soft butter, in pieces
Salt and pepper

Cook the onion, tarragon and vinegar or white wine in a saucepan over a medium heat until the liquid evaporates and the ingredients begin to stick to the bottom. Add the egg yolks beaten with 2 tablespoons of cold water, and whisk in a double boiler until the mixture thickens to a mayonnaise-like consistency. Gradually incorporate the butter, whisking constantly. Season with salt and pepper, to taste.

Blackberry sauce
Makes 1 cup

1 cup blackberries
1/4 cup sugar

Process the blackberries in a blender with 1/2 cup of water and strain into a small saucepan. Add the sugar and cook, stirring until the sugar dissolves. Remove and let stand.

Cheese with fines herbes
Makes 8 tablespoons

1/2 cup cream cheese
1 tablespoon fresh basil, chopped
1 1/2 tablespoons fresh chives, chopped
1 1/2 tablespoons fresh parsley, chopped
Salt and pepper

Place the cream cheese in a bowl. Mix in the chopped fresh herbs and season with salt and pepper, to taste. Keep in the refrigerator until it is time to use.

Clarified butter

Clarified butter is obtained by melting butter so that the fat separates from the impurities and water. To prepare it, skim off the white part that floats on the surface of the resulting liquid and use the remaining, or clarified part, which has a crystalline look and stands up to higher temperatures without getting burnt.

Coconut ice cream
Makes 3 cups

1 cup milk
3/4 cup coconut milk
1/3 cup coconut cream
6 egg yolks
3/4 cup sugar
1 cup cold cream
3/4 cup grated coconut, fresh or dehydrated

Heat the milk, the coconut milk and coconut cream in a saucepan. Mix well. Pour over the egg yolks, whisked with the sugar, and cook over a low heat, stirring until the mixture thickens enough to coat the back of a wooden spoon. Strain into a bowl and set bowl on ice to cool. Whisk the cold cream until it thickens. Mix into the above mixture with the grated coconut.
Transfer to an ice-cream maker and churn according to the manufacturer's instructions.
(Alternatively, you may pour the mixture into a metal bowl, cover with aluminum foil and place in the freezer, whisking every half hour during freezing to break up the ice crystals and obtain a creamier texture.)

Coconut milk

Although coconut milk may be bought in powdered or canned form or in frozen bags, you can prepare it at home, using any of the following procedures: Open the coconut, extract the meat, taking care to remove the brown skin and: process either in a juice extractor or mix in a blender with a bit of boiling water or boiling milk. In the case of desiccated coconut, use the unsweetened kind, hydrate in a sufficient amount of boiling water and blend. Strain in all cases, to finish. Coconut milk is very perishable so it should be consumed quickly and kept refrigerated.

Crèpes batter
12 servings

200 grams/7 oz all-purpose flour, sifted
3 eggs
1 pinch salt
1 teaspoon sugar
3/4 cup milk
1 tablespoon oil or melted butter
1 tablespoon grated orange zest (optional)

Put the flour in a bowl, making a well in the center, and place the beaten eggs, salt and sugar in the well. Stirring with a wooden spoon, add the milk, mixed with 2/3 cup of water, and incorporate the flour, little by little, until a uniform, lump-free mixture is obtained. Incorporate the oil, or the butter, and the grated orange zest. Let stand in the refrigerator for 1 hour. Heat a bit of butter in a slightly-greased non-stick frying pan and add a little of the mixture, swirling the pan with a circular motion so that the bottom is covered with a thin, even layer. Put on the heat and cook for 1 minute. Turn the crèpe over and cook for another minute or until lightly golden. Remove, put on a plate and repeat with the remaining batter.

Dijon vinaigrette
Makes 1/2 cup

1 tablespoon Dijon mustard
1 tablespoon red wine vinegar
1/2 tablespoon nut vinegar
4 1/2 tablespoons olive oil

Dissolve the mustard in the vinegars. Stirring constantly, add the oil, little by little, until it is completely incorporated. Season with salt and pepper, to taste. Add 1/2 tablespoon of water, or the amount that is needed, to obtain the desired consistency.

Fines herbes butter

1/2 cup fresh basil, chopped
1/2 cup fresh parsley, chopped
1 tablespoon chives, chopped
125 grams/4 oz butter, room temperature
Salt and pepper

With a knife, or in the food processor, finely chop the herbs and mix them with the soft butter.
Season with salt and pepper, to taste.

Green curry paste
Makes 4 tablespoons

10 fresh green chili peppers, chopped
1 stalk fresh lemongrass, chopped
2 shallots, chopped
2 garlic cloves, crushed
1 tablespoon fresh ginger, peeled and grated
4 fresh coriander roots, chopped
1 teaspoon coriander seeds
1/2 teaspoon cumin seeds
1/2 teaspoon white peppercorns
1 teaspoon grated lemon zest
2 teaspoons shrimp paste
1 teaspoon salt

Process all of the ingredients in a mortar or blender until a smooth uniform paste is obtained. If necessary, add a little bit of lukewarm water to facilitate blending.

Guava halves poached in syrup
24 halves

12 large, ripe guavas
3 tablespoons lemon juice
2 cups sugar

Wash and peel the guavas. Cut them in half sideways and remove the seeds with a spoon, taking care to keep the shells intact. Cook over high heat with 10 cups of water and the lemon juice for 45 minutes or until tender. Add the sugar. Cook for another 45 minutes. (They should be red and shiny.) Remove from heat and let stand.

Hollandaise sauce
Makes 1 cup

3 egg yolks
1 tablespoon dry white wine
100 grams/3 oz butter, cubed and chilled
1 tablespoon lemon juice
Salt and pepper

Stir the yolks with the wine and cook over a bain marie, stirring until the bottom of the pot is visible and the sauce begins to thicken. Gradually add the butter, stirring constantly until it is completely incorporated. Add the lemon and season with salt and pepper to taste.

Home-made mayonnaise
Makes 1 1/2 cups

1 egg
1 egg yolk
1 tablespoon mustard
1 tablespoon white vinegar
1 tablespoon lemon juice
1 cup vegetable oil
Salt and pepper

Put the egg and yolk in a bowl with the mustard, vinegar and lemon, and mix until creamy. Add the oil in a thin stream, stirring constantly until the mixture thickens. Season with salt and pepper, to taste. This basic mayonnaise may be enriched with additional flavors, such as flavored oils, chili flakes, herbs or spices, and it may also be made in a blender.

Hummus
Makes 1 1/2 cups

300 grams/10 oz canned chickpeas
1/3 cup olive oil
2 1/2 tablespoons tahini paste
1/4 cup lemon juice
Salt and Cayenne pepper

Process all of the ingredients in a blender, adding a little water or juice from the chickpeas, if necessary, until a smooth uniform purée is obtained. Season with salt and pepper, to taste.

Lime marmalade
Makes 3/4 cup

The juice of 3 limes
1 cup sugar
1 tablespoon butter
1 egg, beaten

Boil the lime juice with the sugar and butter. Remove from the heat and add the beaten egg, stirring constantly. Cook until thickened over medium heat. Remove and let stand until cool.

Lime, mint and sesame sauce
Makes 1/2 cup

3 tablespoons lime juice
2 tablespoons soy sauce
2 tablespoons sesame oil
1 tablespoon fresh ginger, grated
1 tablespoon brown sugar
2 tablespoons fresh mint leaves, chopped
1 tablespoon fresh coriander, chopped

Mix all of the ingredients in a non-metallic bowl and serve with fried squids, other seafood or lamb chops.

Mint syrup

2/3 cup sugar
1 cup mint leaves

To prepare the syrup, boil 1 1/2 cups of water with the sugar and cook for 10 minutes or until it begins to thicken. Add the mint leaves. Boil for another minute and remove from the heat. Let cool before serving.

Orange gelée

1/4 cup orange juice
1 tablespoon Cointreau or Grand Marnier
1 1/2 teaspoons gelatin, unflavored
1/2 cup chicken consommé, hot

Mix the orange juice with the Cointreau or Grand Marnier and pour into a small bowl. Sprinkle on a uniform layer of gelatin and let it become spongy. Pour in the hot consommé and stir until dissolved. Let stand for a few minutes and pour into a small shallow baking tin. Refrigerate until set. Cut into small cubes and sprinkle over the pâté.

Pastry cream
Makes 250 grams/8 oz

3 egg yolks
1/4 cup sugar
3 tablespoons all-purpose flour
1 teaspoon cornstarch
1 cup milk
1 teaspoon vanilla extract
1 tablespoon butter

Whisk the yolks with half of the sugar until they are light and creamy. Add the flour and cornstarch, stirring well. Put the milk in a saucepan with the rest of the sugar and the vanilla and bring to a boil. Pour over the egg yolk mixture, stirring constantly. Transfer to a clean saucepan and bring to a boil, constantly stirring until a thick mixture is obtained. Remove from heat. Incorporate the butter and let cream stand in a dish, laying plastic wrap on the surface to prevent a skin from forming.

Pastry for pecan pie
Makes 1 single crust

1 1/4 cups all-purpose flour, sifted
2 tablespoons sugar
1 pinch salt
180 grams/6 oz butter, cubed and chilled
1 egg

Sift the dry ingredients into a bowl, add the butter and rub with your fingertips until the mixture acquires a crumbly consistency or resembles coarse breadcrumbs. Add the egg beaten with 2 1/2 tablespoons of cold water and mix with a flexible bladed knife until the dough just starts to come together. (Add a bit more water if necessary.) Form a ball with your hands, cover in plastic wrap and refrigerate for 1 hour. (Alternatively, prepare the pastry in a food processor, following the same steps and using the pulse button to avoid over-mixing the dough.)

Port and nut fudge sauce
Makes 1 cup

2/3 cup dark brown sugar
1 egg yolk
2 tablespoons port
2 tablespoons cornstarch
4 tablespoons butter, chilled and cubed
2/3 cup nuts, chopped

To prepare the fudge, dissolve the sugar in 1/2 cup of water and heat until a syrup is obtained. Separately mix the egg yolk with the port and cornstarch, adding a bit of the syrup. Pour this mixture over the remaining syrup and heat until thick. Do not boil. Add the chilled butter, stirring little by little until it is completely incorporated. Remove from the heat and add the nuts.

Raspberry sauce
Makes 3/4 cup

1 cup raspberries
2 tablespoons sugar
1/2 teaspoon lemon juice

Process the ingredients in a blender and strain if you wish to eliminate the seeds.

Red curry paste
Makes 4 tablespoons

8 thin dry red chili peppers, seeded and chopped
1 teaspoon coriander seeds
1 teaspoon white peppercorns
2 garlic cloves
2 stalks of lemongrass, the clear part finely chopped
4 coriander roots, finely chopped
1 teaspoon grated lemon zest
1 tablespoon fresh ginger, peeled and grated
2 teaspoons shrimp paste
1 teaspoon salt
1 tablespoon oil

Process all of the ingredients in a mortar, or blender, until a smooth uniform paste is obtained. If necessary, add a little bit of lukewarm water to facilitate blending.

Seafood broth for paella

10 tablespoons olive oil
1 onion, sliced
500 grams/17 oz fish heads
1 bottle dry white wine
1 cup of the shellfish to be used in the paella
Shells from the shellfish of the paella
1 tomato, chopped
1 stalk celery
1/2 carrot
2 tablespoons olive oil
3 bay leaves
1 sprig thyme
1 teaspoon peppercorns
1 sprig coriander
Salt

Heat the oil in a big pot, add the onion and a bit of salt and cook over low heat until it is soft and translucent. Add the fish heads and cook, stirring for 5 minutes. Add the white wine and bring to a boil. Add the shellfish, the shells of the shellfish used in the paella and the rest of the ingredients. Cook, stirring for 5 minutes. Add 15 cups of water and cook for 30 minutes.
Reserve 2 cups of this broth in a separate bowl and let it cool. (It will be used when cooking the onion for the paella.) If the broth evaporates too much during boiling, you may add more water and let it boil again for a few minutes in order to enhance the flavor.
Strain before adding to the paella.

Sesame caramel crunch

2/3 cup sugar
1/3 cup sesame seeds

Pour 1/2 cup of water into a clean heavy-based saucepan, add the sugar in the center and cook over a high heat until it caramelizes and acquires a pronounced amber color. Add the sesame seeds and swirl the saucepan with a circular motion to incorporate. Pour the caramel onto a tin or a silicone baking sheet and let it cool. Cut into pieces and chop finely.

Sweet pastry
Makes 1 single crust

2 cups all-purpose flour, sifted
1/4 cup confectioner's sugar
1 pinch salt
125 grams/4 oz butter, cubed and chilled
1 egg

Sift the dry ingredients into a bowl, add the butter and rub with your fingertips until the mixture acquires a crumbly consistency or resembles coarse breadcrumbs. Put the beaten egg in a measuring cup and add iced water until a level of 110 ml is reached and add to dough, mixing with a flexible bladed knife until the dough just starts to come together. Form a ball with your hands, cover in plastic wrap and refrigerate for at least 30 minutes. (Alternatively, prepare the pastry in a food processor, following the same steps and using the pulse button to avoid over-mixing the dough.)

Tart pastry (*Pâte brisée*)

2 1/4 cups all-purpose flour, sifted
1/2 teaspoon salt
125 grams/4 oz butter, cubed and chilled
1 egg

Sift the dry ingredients into a bowl, add the butter and rub with your fingertips until the mixture acquires a crumbly consistency or resembles coarse breadcrumbs.
Add the egg beaten with 6 to 7 tablespoons of cold water and mix with a flexible bladed knife until the dough just starts to come together. (If necessary, add a bit more water.) Form a ball with your hands, cover in plastic wrap and refrigerate for 30 minutes. (Alternatively, prepare the dough in a food processor, following the same steps and using the pulse button to avoid over-mixing the dough.)

Vanilla ice cream
Makes 2 cups

1 1/2 cups milk
2 vanilla beans
3/4 cup sugar
3 egg yolks
1 cup cream

Pour the milk into a saucepan. Cut the vanilla beans in half, scrape out the seeds and add to the milk.
Add half of the sugar and cook until dissolved. Pour over the eggs, whisked with the rest of the sugar, and cook over low heat, stirring until the mixture thickens enough to coat the back of a wooden spoon.
Strain into a bowl and set bowl on ice to cool. Whisk the cold cream until it thickens. Add cream to the above mixture. Transfer to an ice-cream maker and churn according to the manufacturer's instructions.
(Alternatively, you may pour the mixture into a metal bowl, cover with aluminum foil and place in the freezer, whisking every half hour during freezing to break up the ice crystals and obtain a creamier texture.)

Wine sauce for turkey
Makes 3 cups

3 tablespoons butter
1/4 cup flour
3 cups chicken stock
1 sprig thyme
1 cup dry white wine
Salt and pepper

Melt the butter in a saucepan, add the flour and cook over low heat, stirring until the mixture is browned. Slowly add the stock, stirring constantly. Add the thyme, cook for another 20 minutes and reserve.
Separately, pour the cup of wine into the roasting pan where you cooked the turkey and place it on the stove. Cook for 5 minutes to deglaze and add to the reserved sauce. Cook a little longer, until the sauce slightly thickens. Season to taste with salt and pepper. Strain and serve hot.

Glossary

Al dente: an Italian term that means 'firm to the bite' and indicates the desired point of cooking of pasta, rice or vegetables. It means that the food is just about cooked. Cooked pasta should have just a touch of resistance to the bite and be tender without any hint of rawness. Vegetables that are cooked until they are al dente have a firm, crisp texture.

Alfajor: pastry sandwich dusted with confectioner's sugar and rolled in grated coconut.

Amaretto: a sweet Italian liqueur made from almonds

Aspic: a flavored jelly of strong consistency, which is frequently chopped or set in a smooth layer over pâté.

Baba ghanoush: name given to a purée made from eggplant, tahini, olive oil, lemon and garlic, typical of Middle Eastern cuisine, which is accompanied by pita bread.

Bain Marie: a system for gentle cooking where the food is cooked in a double boiler on the stove or in a roasting pan half-filled with water in the oven.

Balsamic vinegar: made from the natural fermentation process of pressing Trebbiano grapes that grow on the hills around Modena in Italy. The traditional production of this vinegar involves aging over a number of years in successive casks of different woods, which progressively add their different aromas and flavors to the vinegar. A traditional vinegar takes 12 years to mature and a fully aged one up to 25 years. However, cheaper industrial varieties are also available.

Blue cheese: a popular variety of cheese with a strong flavor, made from cow's or goat's milk and known for its taste and aroma, as well as its special texture and blue-green veins of mold. Among the best-known ones are Gorgonzola, of Italian origin; Stilton, of English origin, and the Danish Danablu.

Boconccini: small balls of Mozzarella cheese, which are almost always sold packed in water or whey, and used for different kinds of snacks.

Brie cheese: a soft, white French cheese, native to the region of Brie in France.

Bucattini: a long, tubular pasta that comes in different diameters. Its hollow center allows it to be impregnated with different flavors.

Cajeta: a thick milk caramel made from caramelized sugar and milk—usually goat's milk, though today it is also made from cow's milk. Popular in Mexico, cajeta is a dessert in itself, although it may also accompany ice cream, tortillas, crèpes or fruits.

Camembert cheese: the most popular of the soft white French cheeses, it is made from cow's milk. Legend has it that Napoleon named it in honor of the town where he tried it for the first time.

Chantilly cream: sweetened, vanilla-flavored, whipped cream used for desserts and puddings.

Churro: a kind of sweet fritter, similar to a crueller, made from a strip of fried dough and heavily sprinkled with sugar. It sometimes has a sweet filling of custard, chocolate or *dulce de leche*.

Chutney: typical to India, the chutney is usually a spicy mixture of fruits, herbs and seasonings. Popular throughout the world, chutneys are excellent and creative accompaniments, not only to Indian dishes, but also those from other countries.

Clafoutis: a fruit-filled custard that originated in Limousin, France's cherry-producing region, this dessert consists of a preparation of fresh fruit covered with batter that is baked and served hot, generally accompanied by cream. Traditionally filled with cherries, clafoutis adapts well to any fresh fruit in season; strawberries, blueberries and raspberries substitute well.

Coconut cream: a thick, sugared extract, pressed and processed from fresh coconut, and heat treated to preserve. It may be bought in canned form, and is used for desserts and cocktails.

Coconut milk: coconut milk is not the liquid from inside the nut, but the extract of freshly grated or dehydrated coconut flesh.

Cointreau: a brandy-based liqueur of French origin, whose flavor is obtained from the peel of sweet and bitter oranges

Corn syrup: sweet, thick syrup made from maize starch and used in the preparation of desserts.

Creole potato: a small, round, yellow variety of potato, with a soft pulp, grown in the Andes.

Crumble: a dough made from flour and butter that is crumbled into pieces with the fingers to resemble breadcrumbs and then baked. It is often used as a topping over fresh fruit desserts, but may also be prepared for savory dishes.

Curry: name for the aromatic and generally spicy mixture of various spices, such as cumin, coriander, chilies and turmeric, that is widely used in the cuisine of India, Thailand and Indonesia.

Dashi: a basic ingredient of Japanese cooking, dashi is a soup stock. The most common kind is made from a combination of dried kelp (*konbu*) and shavings from dried bonito fillets. It is sold in a concentrated form, whose generic name is *dashi-no-moto*, which is instantly prepared by dissolving in water.

Dijon mustard: this famous mustard is made from mustard paste and white wine. It has a paler color than other mustards and is named after the French city where it originated.

Dulce de leche: a milk caramel, obtained through the concentration, by heat, of cow's milk solids with sugar. In Colombia it is known as *arequipe*.

Feta cheese: a soft white Greek cheese, originally made from goat's or sheep's milk, though it is also made today from cow's milk.

Filo: also spelled phyllo, is a versatile pastry dough, stretched into paper-thin sheets and used extensively in Middle Eastern sweets. It is sold in a prepared form.

Fonduta: an Italian-style fondue, made from a mixture of melted cheese (usually Fontina) and wine into which foods such as bread and vegetables are dipped. Typical to Northern Italy, it may also be used as a sauce for vegetables.

Garam masala: a typical spice found in Indian cuisine, it is composed of a mixture of up to 12 different varieties of spices, which are roasted and ground. Although there are as many types of garam masala as chefs, they generally include chilies, cinnamon, fennel, black pepper, cumin, nutmeg, coriander, cardamom and cloves.

Goldenberry: small fruit of the Andes, whose local name is *uchuva*. *Uchuvas* are the shape and size of marbles, have a golden color and are protected by papery husks.

Gorgonzola cheese: see Blue cheese.

Graibe: delicate cookie made with clarified butter and topped with an almond. Popular in Middle Eastern cuisine.

Grand Marnier: cognac-based French liqueur, with a taste obtained from bitter oranges

Gruyère cheese: a French cheese, with a firm, smooth texture and a nutty flavor. The variety with many small holes is known as *gruyère de Comté*, while that without holes is known as *gruyère de Beaufort*.

Juliennes: thin sticks of food, especially greens, also called matchsticks. The food is cut with a knife or mandoline into even slices and then into strips.

Mâche: a wild lettuce, of Mediterranean origin, also called *doucette*, with small round leaves that may be used for salads. It is also cultivated in France, Italy, and the U.S.

Mandoline: a hand-operated machine used for cutting and slicing fruits and vegetables. This kitchen utensil has a variety of adjustable blades that enable the tool to make precise cuts in firm fruits and vegetables.

Mangosteen: a fruit similar in size and shape to a lime, which is brownish purple on the outside and has a sweet white, jelly-like flesh, similar to a lychee.

Mascarpone cheese: a thick Italian cream cheese, native to the region of Lombard. It is used to enrich sauces or desserts, and may also be sweetened and flavored to eat on its own.

Mirin: a liquid-type seasoning, made in Japan from *mochi gome* (sweet glutinous rice). Its sugar and alcohol contents give it a distinctive flavor. It is only used for culinary purposes in Japan, or ceremonially in the Japanese New Year's celebrations.

Mozzarella cheese: one of the most popular Italian cheeses, it is traditionally made with the *pasta filata* method, by which the curd is submerged in the whey and then hand-stretched to the desired consistency. Originally made from buffalo milk, today it is made with cow's milk. Mild and creamy in taste.

Nori: thin, crisp, dark sheets of a dried seaweed, native to the seas of Japan, roasted under a heat lamp and used to wrap up sushi and rice balls, among other foods. It is a source of high-grade protein, calcium, carotene and iron.

Panela: pure natural cane sugar, without additives, concentrated by boiling into a hard block. It is known as rock sugar or brown sugar loaf in English.

Parmesan cheese: hard, grainy cheese extensively used in Italian cuisine, made from non-fat or low-fat cow's-milk. Possibly the best known Italian cheese, it is almost always grated over dishes.

Prosciutto: a delicate air-dried, salt-cured Italian ham, which is best when sliced paper thin.

Raclette cheese: a cheese native to Switzerland that is made from cow's milk and is similar to Gruyère in both texture (semi-firm and dotted with small holes) and flavor (mellow and nutty). The same name is used for a traditional wintertime dish in Switzerland, in which melted slices of Raclette cheese are served over sliced potatoes and seasoned with ground pepper and paprika.

Radicchio: a member of the chicory family, of Italian origin, with bright red leaves with white veins. Famous since ancient times, Radicchio is peppery, crunchy, and bitter, which makes it excellent for salads.

Ramekin: a small, straight-sided round ceramic dish. Ramekins are ovenproof and are ideal for preparing soufflés or custards. They are sold both in casserole size and for individual servings.

Risotto: term used for an Italian cooking technique for native Italian rice, which involves stirring hot liquid little by little into the rice for about 20 minutes to produce a texture of creamy sauce around rice grains which are cooked *al dente*. Risottos are known for their variety of flavors and the creative incorporation of diverse ingredients.

Sesame oil: a dark thick oil made from sesame seeds.

Soy sauce: the most common cooking and table sauce of Japan, China and the rest of the Orient. There are innumerable types and varieties of soy sauce.

Sumac: a dark red powdered spice, made from the berry of the sumac bush. Highly esteemed in the Middle East for its citric taste, sumac is used in the preparation of meats, bread and salads.

Tahini: a thick paste made from sesame seeds, and very popular in the Middle East. It serves as the base to prepare a wide variety of other foods, such as hummus.

Tapenade: native to the Provence region of France, this is a rich, soft spread, usually made from a mixture of capers, anchovies, ripe olives, olive oil and lemon. Tapenade is traditionally spread on bread, but it can also be added to cooked pasta, fish, meat, raw greens or used in canapés.

Tataki: Japanese method of cooking in which the outer surface of seasoned and oiled beef or tuna is flame-burned in a frying pan or grill to seal in its flavor: it forms an outer ring of cooked meat and a rare, juicy center.

Tempura: Japanese method of deep frying fish, meats or vegetables dipped in a light batter of sifted flour with egg and water or soda water.

Turmeric: this distinctive bright yellow spice is a member of the ginger family, and fresh turmeric has a very similar appearance to fresh ginger - it is a light brown knobby root. Fresh turmeric is not widely available and most turmeric that is grown in India, China, the West Indies and Africa is dried, ground and sold as a powder. It has a slight peppery aroma and a musky taste. It is one of the basic ingredients for many curries.

Uchuva: see "Goldenberry".

Vermicelli: very thin, round noodles, also known as cellophane noodles, made from Mung bean flour. They become transparent when submerged in boiling water.

Wasabi: a green root, indigenous to Japan, which, in prepared form, is the traditional spicy condiment of Japanese cuisine. Though it is sometimes called Japanese horse-radish, it really belongs to the mustard family.

Wonton: comparable to the Italian ravioli, the Chinese wonton consists of a thin wrapper of dough filled with meat, seafood or vegetables. Wontons may be cooked in water, steamed or deep fried. In addition to being used in soups, wontons are served as snacks with diverse sauces. Packets of prepared wrappers are widely available.

Index of ingredients

Almonds, 18, 28, 37, 132, 162, 176, 179, 180, 217, 218
Amaretto, 128, 158, 162, 207, 217
Anchovy, 46, 60, 151, 219
Apple, 86, 104, 180, 199
Apricot, 37, 124, 128, 129, 131
Artichoke, 193
Asparagus, 66
Aspic, 197, 208, 217
Avocado, 53, 61
Baby banana, 159
Bacon, 99
Banana, 139
Basil, 60, 62, 74, 111, 116, 144, 151, 170, 210, 213
Beer, 128
Beet-root, 170
Black sesame seeds, 147
Blackberry, 86, 158, 159, 162, 168, 169, 215
Boconccini cheese balls, 60
Brie cheese, 50, 202, 218
Broccoli, 69
Bucattini pasta, 112, 217
Cactus fruit, 141
Cajeta, 176, 217
Camembert cheese, 66, 218
Capers, 46, 60, 151, 219
Cardamom, 44, 81, 105, 124, 132, 205, 218
Carrot, 82, 115, 132, 199, 207
Cashew nuts, 73, 115

Cayenne pepper, 54, 209
Champagne, 128
Chantilly cream, 204, 217
Cheese,
    Blue cheese, 82, 86, 189, 218
    Brie cheese, 50, 202, 218
    Camembert cheese, 66, 218
    Edam cheese, 99
    Feta cheese, 60, 218
    Gorgonzola cheese, 112, 218
    Gruyère cheese, 85, 86, 99, 218
    Raclette cheese, 86, 218
Chicken liver, 197
Chicken, 23, 60, 61, 75, 78, 81, 82, 85, 115, 116, 183, 186, 197, 199, 208
Chickpeas, 209
Chili,
    Chili powder, 21, 81
    Dry chili flakes, 73, 151
    Green chili pepper, 53
    Red chili pepper, 18, 78, 121, 154
    Sweet chili sauce, 186
Chocolate,
    Bittersweet, 179
    Dark chocolate, 179
    White chocolate, 96, 159
Chocolate liqueur, 179
Clam, 78, 154, 190
Clarified butter, 28, 50, 152, 210
Cocoa, 179, 203

Coconut milk, 23, 34, 53, 62, 78, 95, 168, 202, 209, 210, 218
Coconut, 18, 23, 29, 34, 38, 46, 53, 62, 78, 95, 131, 168, 202, 203, 209, 210, 217
Coffee, 138, 183, 189, 203, 205, 218
Cognac, 121, 189, 218
Cointreau, 105, 197, 199, 208, 217
Condensed milk, 204, 205
Consommé (stock),
    Beef stock, 193
    Chicken stock, 23, 60, 61, 78, 82, 85, 116, 183, 199, 208, 213
    Fish stock, 121
Coriander seeds, 81, 212
Corn syrup, 135, 174, 207, 217
Cornstarch, 21, 29, 37, 38, 96, 102, 115, 121, 122, 179, 208, 214
Couscous, 60
Crab claws, 152, 154
Crab, 152, 154
Cranberries, 159
Crayfish, 121, 154
Cream cheese, 118, 213, 218
Cream of tartar, 38, 179
Croutons, 50, 82, 85
Crumble, 162, 217
Cucumber, 111
Curry powder, 61, 81

Dashi stock, 186, 217
Dates, 37, 170, 179, 180
Dijon Mustard, 46, 57, 144, 187, 215, 218
Dill, 118, 141
Earl Grey tea, 128
Eggplant, 194, 217
Essence of roses, 37
Feta cheese, 60, 218
Filo pastry dough, 50, 217
Fish sauce, 18, 53, 152, 186
French bread, 86
Fresh salmon, 108, 141
Fudge, 180, 208, 217
Garam masala spice, 131, 217
Ginger, 45, 78, 81, 108, 129, 131, 186, 212, 215
Goldenberry, 129, 138
Gorgonzola cheese, 82, 112, 218
Graham crackers, 203
Graibe cookies with almonds, 28, 218
Grand Marnier, 199, 208, 218
Granola, 138
Grape leaves, 60, 65
Grapefruit, 18, 129, 138
Green (snap) beans, 73, 154
Green curry paste, 62, 212
Green plantain, 104
Green tea, 159
Grouper, 62, 154
Gruyère cheese, 85, 86, 99
Guavas, 161, 207
Heavy cream, 66, 69, 82, 96, 116, 118, 121, 132, 135,

159, 161, 165, 174, 183, 190, 197, 209, 217
Honey, 99, 199, 203, 214
Hot chili sauce, 187, 202
Hummus, 54, 65, 209
Jalapeño chili pepper, 61
Jasmine petals, 45
Ketchup, 115, 187, 214
Lamb chops, 187
Lamb, 187
Lemongrass, 23, 75, 111, 129, 212
Linguini pasta, 151
Lychees, 34
Macadamia nuts, 159
Mâche, 218
Mango, 105, 186
Mangosteen fruit, 37
Maple syrup, 99, 161, 214
Marshmallow, 44
Mascarpone cheese, 140, 218
Milk caramel, 29, 41, 176
Mirin seasoning, 108, 186, 218
Mozzarella cheese, 86, 144, 217, 218
Mushrooms, 183
Mussels, 190
Nectarine, 129
Nori seaweed, 73, 108, 218
Nutmeg, 69, 86, 91, 139, 180, 202, 218
Olive, 60, 151, 219
Orange blossom extract, 15, 37, 135
Orange gelée, 197, 208, 217

Orange, 41, 82, 102, 111, 128, 129, 135, 162, 176, 180, 197, 208, 210, 217, 218
Oregano, 121, 151
Parmesan cheese, 90, 118, 218
Passion fruit, 96
Peach, 129, 140
Peanut butter, 202
Peanut, 18, 124, 202
Pear, 74, 104, 129
Peasant bread, 82
Pecan, 174, 211
Pickled ginger, 108
Pie crust (pâte brisée), 66, 213
Pine nuts, 176, 218
Pineapple, 62
Pistachio, 37, 140
Poppy seeds, 139
Port wine, 179, 180, 208, 218
Potato, 74, 81, 90, 91, 118
Prawns, 54, 111, 121, 122, 154
Prosciutto ham, 170
Prunes, 180, 187
Pumpkin, 112
Radicchio lettuce, 144, 219
Raspberry, 159, 162, 214
Red curry paste, 152, 212
Red snapper, 65
Rib roast, 148
Rice,
    Arborio rice, 23
    Basmati rice, 81, 124
    Parboiled rice, 154

Rose petals, 45, 103, 158
Saffron threads, 103, 104, 121, 154, 190
Sea salt, 47, 54, 121, 141
Sechuan pepper (pink peppercorn), 54, 60
Sesame seeds, 21, 73, 108, 147, 159, 187, 208, 215, 217, 219
Sherry, 85, 148
Shrimp paste, 212
Shrimp, 154, 212
Sirloin steaks, 189
Sirloin, 148
Smoked salmon, 66, 118
Sour cream, 46, 60, 61, 118, 217
Soy sauce, 108, 147, 152, 186, 199, 219
Spare ribs, 187
Spearmint, 18, 54, 60, 95, 129, 141, 161, 186
Squash, 78
Squid, 21, 154, 215
Star anise, 199
String beans, 148
Sumac, 54, 60, 219
Sweet chili sauce, 186
Tahini, 194, 209, 217, 219
Tangerine, 128
Tarragon, 148, 214
Tea, 93, 128, 159, 205, 218
Tenderloin steaks, 186
Tequila, 105, 176
Tomato, 60, 61, 81, 115, 116, 121, 144, 151, 154,

171, 187, 190, 193, 207, 214
Triple sec, 34
Tuna fish, 73, 147, 219
Turkey, 199, 213
Turmeric, 217, 219
Turmeric, 81, 217, 219
Vanilla ice cream, 161, 162, 176, 209
Vegetable stock, 23
Vermicelli noodles, 18, 219
Vinegar,
    Balsamic vinegar, 144, 219
    Cider vinegar, 131, 214
    Nut vinegar, 215
    Red wine vinegar, 215
    Rice wine vinegar, 18, 108, 115, 152, 186, 187
Vodka, 105, 158, 168
Wasabi, 73, 147, 219
Watercress, 66
Watermelon, 158
Whisky, 189
White fish, 53, 62, 154
White radish, 104
White wine, 78, 85, 86, 116, 121, 129, 151, 183, 190, 197, 199, 207, 213, 214, 215, 218
Wonton, 116, 147, 219
Worcestershire sauce, 148, 187, 214
Yogurt, 81, 219